GARDEN FLOWERS IN COLOUR

Garden Flowers

in Colour

Brian and Valerie Proudley

BLANDFORD   PRESS

POOLE   DORSET

First published in 1979
Copyright © 1979 Blandford Press Ltd
Link House, West Street
Poole, Dorset BH15 1LL

ISBN 0 7137 0911 1

Set in 10 on 11 pt Monophoto Imprint by Keyspools Ltd,
Golborne, Lancashire.
Printed in Great Britain
by Fletcher & Son Ltd, Norwich
Colour plates printed by Sackville Press, Billericay.

CONTENTS

METRIC CONVERSION TABLE

Dimensions (approx.)

0.3 m = 1 ft	1.5 m = 5 ft
0.5 m = 1½ ft	2 m = 6 ft
0.6 m = 2 ft	2.5 m = 8 ft
0.7 m = 2 ft	3 m = 10 ft
0.8 m = 2½ ft	1 m = 39.4 in
1 m = 3 ft	1 m^2 = 10.8 sq ft

1 cm = ½ in	15 cm = 6 in
2 cm = ¾ in	18 cm = 7 in
3 cm = 1 in	20 cm = 8 in
4 cm = 1½ in	23 cm = 9 in
5 cm = 2 in	25 cm = 10 in
6 cm = 2¼ in	28 cm = 11 in
7 cm = 2¾ in	30 cm = 12 in
8 cm = 3 in	35 cm = 14 in
9 cm = 3½ in	38 cm = 15 in
10 cm = 4 in	40 cm = 16 in
11 cm = 4½ in	45 cm = 18 in
12 cm = 4¾ in	50 cm = 20 in
13 cm = 5 in	60 cm = 24 in
14 cm = 5½ in	70 cm = 29 in

Temperatures

0C = 32F	20C = 68F
5C = 41F	25C = 77F
10C = 50F	30C = 86F
15C = 59F	35C = 95F

ACKNOWLEDGEMENTS

Although many of the photographs are of flowers grown in our own garden we have been able to enlarge the range included by taking pictures in different places in several countries. Our grateful thanks is extended to all who have assisted by allowing us access to their gardens.

Special thanks are due to The Crown Estate Commissioners, Savill Garden, The Great Park, Windsor, Berkshire; The Curator, Royal Botanic Garden, Kew, Richmond, Surrey; Mr and Mrs R. Kingham, Oak Beam Cottage, Coed-y-paen, Pontypool, South Wales; Mr George Osmond, Archfield Nursery, Wickwar, Gloucestershire; The Director, Royal Horticultural Society, Wisley, Ripley, Surrey; The Secretary, Seventh Day Adventist Hospital, St Heliers, Auckland, New Zealand.

INTRODUCTION

The topic of this book, garden flowers, is a wide one. As everyone knows it covers so very much more than simply the seed-raised plants or herbaceous perennials described. The first subjects to consider when planning a garden full of colour and interest must be trees, shrubs and climbers. Trees, as well as providing shade impart a sense of maturity to the garden. Most shrubs flower delightfully and give shelter too. House walls and fences need climbers and twiners to clothe and decorate. Then there are the roses and bulbs which provide a richness of seasonal colour not to be ignored when planning the garden display. After you have planted a selection of the foregoing in numbers relative to the size of your garden will be the time to consider some of the other garden flowers.

Perhaps extra words should have been inserted into the title of this book to make it *Our Favourite*, or *Familiar Garden Flowers*, for we were asked to choose and describe a selection of garden flowers which we consider to be of the greatest value particularly to new gardeners. Naturally enough we have included all of our favourites – we hope that they are yours too!

For a fine display arrange to have special beds or borders planted with biennials or herbaceous perennials, certain sorts of these can also find homes in light woodland shade, yet others by the streamside. When raised at home annuals provide a mass of colour quickly at small cost. Use these either alone or in mixed beds. Once again, annuals raised initially in seed trays can be used in patio planters and window boxes near the house. These containers need plenty of variety to add interest. Ring the changes with low cost annuals!

The Soil

The creation of soil is a continuing process something which is going on all the time. Decayed plant materials as well as the physical action of sun, frost and wind on the rocks all play their part. It is an awesome thought to consider that all terrestial life is dependent on this thin layer of material which we know as soil. Landsmen usually refer to their soil as being light, medium or heavy. This is oversimplifying things of course for very many different types of soil are covered within these three groups. In fact, we have personally gardened in various parts of England: stony Hertfordshire, where small stones virtually replaced the soil, in the Chilterns where the ground can be almost white with the quantity of chalk present; in Oxfordshire and the Cotswold Hills where there are many beautiful gardens. We consider ourselves fortunate to have been able to have worked in some of them even though the earth can change to plastic mud in wet weather only to become concrete-like when dry. The soil often contains masses of sharp flints to add to problems.

Our Gloucestershire garden was on the side of a steep valley, no doubt carved out over the years by the action of a tumbling stream which had also carried down the deep reddish coloured sand from the rounded hills above. In New Zealand we have experienced what it is like to be able to dig soil composed of pumice so free-draining that one can work on it minutes after heavy rain. In Continental Europe there are places where the water table can be regulated – very useful both in winter and summer. In all probability it is the North American sub-continent which has the greatest variation of all, both in soil types and the wide ranging temperatures encountered. All of this leads us to wonder how it is that although there are great differences of soil the appearance of individual garden plants is virtually identical the world over? The different grades of soil will certainly require individual treatment but the end result will be the same provided the plants' nutrient requirements are met.

Chapter 1 is about the planning and theory and Chapter 2 deals with the soil and actual work needed to grow lovely flowers.

The Plants

It is possible to choose plants which once sited can remain in place for years with the minimum of attention. Others need manuring, staking, cutting back and so on. When it comes to the actual work involved in raising garden flowers (Chapter 3) it will be found that these too fall into different groups and depending on whether they are annual, biennial or perennial plants. Annuals and biennials are always raised from seed. After flowering, their life cycle over, they die; annuals complete their cycle in one season, biennials in two. During the first year biennials grow into leafy plants with an established root system, their second and final season is occupied with flowering and seed bearing. Perennial or perpetual plants have a woody portion which remains each season. From this rootstock springs the annual leafy growth which flowers and normally bears seed every year.

Although a great many perennial plants can be grown from seeds it should be borne in mind that almost all of these plants are 'clones'. This term is used for plants that have been derived from a single original by vegetative means (cuttings of stem or root or divisions) only. Consequently these do not 'breed true' and seedlings cannot be relied upon to exhibit the same characteristics as their named parents. Because of seedling variation, most of their desired features are lost in succeeding generations. You may wonder how a clone or cultivar of a perennial plant can come about. Often these originally would have been seedlings themselves, so it is true to say that a new seedling although different need not necessarily be inferior to its parents. Many of the best cultivars of certain plants e.g. delphiniums, are the result of deliberate cross-pollination by skilled hybridists. Many hundreds of seedlings may be discarded before the propagator is satisfied that the features he is seeking are combined in a particular plant. This is then increased by the vegetative means mentioned earlier before being offered for sale. Some plants as well as being selected seedlings, such as named chrysanthemums, originate when a keen-eyed nurseryman or gardener spots a colour variation in a particular branch or shoot. These are rooted and if they prove to be distinct enough are marketed when sufficient stocks can be built up. These colour variants will remain true to the original 'sport' unless they mutate again – an unlikely occurrence. The attractive variegated leaved plants such as the colourful 'geraniums' are another example of how mutations can increase the range of garden flowers. All of these will remain true to type providing they are increased by vegetative means only. Many, especially of the more common border plants, are easily increased by splitting the old clumps into several pieces. Although kind friends will proffer such plants to the owner of a new garden, and they may be gratefully received at the time, beware that these gifts by their very nature do not romp over the ground swallowing up the more choice subjects in their wake.

We always think that well prepared soil warrants a careful selection of plants. If the owner of a new garden cannot immediately run to the often considerable cost of the many items needed, we would like to suggest that after they have planted their trees and shrubs the beds are filled with hardy annuals that can be sown where they are to flower. The permanent border plants can go in at some future date. When the time comes to consider planting and the choice of just what goes in, it is worth remembering the saying 'Quality does not cost – it pays!'.

Problems

The common pests and diseases which the flower gardener is likely to encounter is the closing topic of the first section. This is a short chapter not so much because it is an unimportant subject but more that garden plants once established do not as a rule suffer from too many problems. Pests and diseases there are of course, so as well as taking precautions a watchful eye should be kept open for insects that disfigure and diseases that weaken or kill.

1 TODAY'S FLOWER GARDEN

Not too many years ago virtually every suburban villa in Britain had its twice yearly display of bedding plants. In the summer months scarlet geraniums, white marguerite daisies and blue lobelias vied with giant dahlias, purple petunias and the like for a place in the planting scheme. Springtime would see the emergence of bulbs neat in their rows, wallflowers, sweet williams in bright array together with all those other flowers which made up their spring 'display'. Public parks and botanic gardens managed the most elaborate schemes of carpet bedding which involved the setting out of thousands of tiny plants each one playing its part in building up a dense mat of colour. Also used were masses of tender and tropical perennials to provide a riot of colour much to the delight and taste of the visitors.

Although gardens both private and public are still bright with flowers, the trend today is away from the tender subjects which require much time both to raise and tend. Many of the easily raised annuals are now used together with low maintenance border perennials and shrubs. Much of the rigid formality of earlier days has now gone leaving us with more flexibility in the design of the modern garden. Formal bedding-out is still done by some, of course, but generally on a much-reduced scale.

As mentioned, the first consideration regarding planting should be for shelter or shade and the trees, hedges and shrubs which provide a permanent foundation planting. Once these have been planted, or provision made to do so later, it will be time to consider where the flowers are to go. At this stage it might be in order to suggest that unless the new gardener is prepared to be reasonably systematic in his approach to planning it is doubtful whether complete success will ever be achieved. A knowledge of environmental conditions such as the nature of the soil, aspect,

12

etc., plus time spent on studying the material available for planting, its likes and dislikes, will do much to confirm just what will succeed in your situation.

Work to a plan

The area to be planted can be measured, then a rough planting plan drawn up using a piece of graph paper for simplicity. One does not have to show where every last plant has to go at this stage, just where the main planting is to take place. Later, once the soil has been prepared, more detail can be added. The plan then becomes a working guide to point to planting positions when the young flower plants arrive.

Importance of correct selection of planting material

Most plants have a built-in adaptability to different types of soil also to varying conditions. This does not mean, however, that all kinds grow everywhere especially when it comes to a shady spot or the amount of moisture present during the growing season. Often choice subjects which prefer a damp soil in shade are developed from species which naturally inhabit woodland or shady mountainsides. In the garden select a position in dappled shade for these. Most woodland species will grow in part shade, but remember that they require adequate moisture particularly during the spring and early summer when they are in active growth. Dry shade in the garden is perhaps the most difficult position of all to fill. Even here it will be found that there are several kinds of plants which flourish if kept well watered during their initial season. If you are like us and do not enjoy the task of staking (and it seems there are a few who do), then for preference choose sturdy lower growing cultivars rather than tall-stemmed sorts that require supporting. Certain plants such as the tall delphinium will always require a cane to each stem. We forgive these for the unique splendour they bring to the summer garden.

Group plants for the best effect

If in summer your soil does not dry out too quickly, added height can be obtained by mounding the bed slightly towards the centre. Unless the area to be planted is very small indeed, groups of the same cultivar should be planted together rather than a mixture of all kinds. This provides a bold splash of one colour much more noticeable than a kaleidoscope of many. Three specimens of the more vigorous kinds should be the minimum planted, increasing to five smaller ones at the edge of the bed. Ample spacing must be allowed for development during the growing season. This applies equally between groups of plants as well as individuals. Where plants are crowded much of the grouping effect will be lost. Another point to bear in mind when making a selection is to choose those plants which require similar growing conditions. Not all border plants grow at the same speed. For this reason keep groups of the more vigorous upright growers separate from the slow-growing, spreading kinds. A change in texture or form is also a desirable feature. To achieve this break up billowy masses of *Aster*, *Gypsophila* etc. with the architectural spires of *Acanthus, Aconitum* and delphiniums. Many of the colourful rock or alpine plants are really tiny shrublets. Apart from their normal home in rock gardens these are fine for small, well-drained, permanant beds where by reason of their compact nature they reduce work to a minimum. In all design the aim should be a pleasing balance between contrast and harmony.

Herbaceous perennials flower naturally over a long season. Lean times can be complemented by using seed raised plants and bulbs to fill any gaps in flowering. Some people prefer to enjoy a really colourful display for, say, the spring months up to early summer when every plant will be in flower. The short seasonal display over, interest is then switched away from that particular border for the remainder of the year. This can be done with planning and can be most effective especially if you have room in the garden for other such borders. For the summer months a grey or silver border with groups of long flowering pinks added to provide blooms could be one such alternative. The main problem in a bed designed for a long display is the fact that bare patches devoid of interest are left when early flowers are over. Once more, a little forethought can help to eliminate this. If for example late flowering Michaelmas daises (*Aster*) are placed next to a group of lupins these will develop to cover the gap in flowering. When it comes to colour combinations most people will have their own preferences. Three well-known colour schemes for flowers are blue with yellow; white with red; and pink with blue.

Herbaceous borders

The traditional design of the 'English Border', as it is known, is long, comparatively narrow in width and normally has a clipped hedge of yew, or in the worst examples, privet, as a background. Many famous borders still in existence are double with a grass or gravel walk between them; several fine examples may be seen in various parts of the country. There are drawbacks however when it comes to scaling down this style of border in today's smaller garden. The biggest problem is maintenance of both the border itself and also the hedge used as backdrop. In addition unless the border is very wide the plants at the back tend to get drawn up due to the hedge blocking out much of the light.

'Island' beds

Island beds can be described as irregular shaped borders usually set well out in the lawn, if not then at least they are accessible from all sides. This style of planting was largely initiated by Mr Alan Bloom of Bressingham Norfolk, the author and nursery-man whose firm as well as introducing many splendid new plants to gardeners also produces them in vast quantities. In his Dell Garden he has successfully demonstrated that when borders are planted in this way the plants not only grow more naturally but cultivation is easier too. Another advantage over the one-sided border is that the island bed can be viewed from all sides. Mr Bloom has found that the ideal height for the tallest plants which occupy the centre part of the bed should not exceed half of its width. This means that in a border three metres wide no plants which attain much more than 1.5m in height can be selected. In the traditional one-sided border the taller plants must be situated at the rear or a top-heavy appearance will result.

Modern mixed borders

Another style of planting which has gained in popularity in recent years is one that combines shrubs and perennial plants. Here the shrubs provide permanence and background height. The flowers contribute the main display of colour each year and also a change in texture and form. The flexibility of these informal borders suits today's taste for variety with low upkeep. There are many flowers particularly suited to this arrangement and which require the minimum of attention such as peonies, *Bergenia* and *Astilbe*. Once planted, these can remain undisturbed for many seasons. Bulbs, lilies particularly, look well when placed in groups here and there through these borders.

Instant colour from seed

The so-called hardy annuals can be sown directly in the soil where they are to flower. They can be used to fill in gaps in permanent beds or given a sunny space of their own. These plants revel in the sun but that does not mean that they like a dry place. Where the ground becomes dust-like you will find that the display is short lived. The design for a bed of these colourful gems extends as far as your imagination. There is such variety available today that it would be possible to vary the colours, and shapes for year after year without repeating the same 'design' twice. Annuals are among the easiest of plants to grow. Their requirements are simple cultivation of the soil with a light dressing of bone dust or superphosphate of lime. Some peat or old manure may be dug in prior to sowing but do not use the latter if in a fresh state or too powerful a fertiliser for these. There must be few gardeners (including ourselves) who have not heeded the latter requirements, the result being masses of lush green floppy growth then after that few flowers to show for all your efforts.

Half-hardy annuals

As their name suggests half-hardy annuals are frost tender and require protection in their early stages and cannot be planted out until danger of frost is past. Hardy annuals raised under glass have also to receive similar treatment. As plants, their flowering performance in a normal season is predictable and growth even. Their place in the garden is usually for filling small formal beds. Once again, whether purchased or home-raised seedlings are used, exciting colour scenes can be worked out. Perhaps you will choose to plant a bed with a single type such as bedding dahlias? These will provide a kaleidoscope of lovely colours for months. For sheer amount of flowers, although admittedly in rather brash colours, the newer F_1 French and African marigolds are real value for money. At the time of writing this we have a small bed of these plants in three sorts and they have been flowering for literally months. There are brilliant orange French for the main colour with the rounded yellow globes of the Africans here and there as dot plants. An edging of tiny flowered tagetes completes the design. Should you have a spot which is cool, moist and lightly shaded the newer kinds of *Impatiens* either in mixed or self colours will be a good choice to make.

Biennials

Biennial plants are raised in a spare plot for their first season then transplanted later to the place they will occupy when they flower. Depending on the species they will either be used for spring flowering bedding or filling spaces in summer borders.

Wallflowers are favourites in several countries including Britain. They associate well with bulbs, particularly Narcissi and tulips. A bed of *Myosotis* (perhaps better known as forget-me-not), a few mixed colour wallflowers, together with tulips dotted here and there make a charming sight as the brighter colours are emphasised against the pale blue ground. Then there are the polyanthus and coloured primroses. What a pretty bed or edging these make as they welcome the spring. Both blend well with *Myosotis* and tulips. As well as the usual places try these in tubs or window boxes.

Where the ground is to be used for a main summer bedding plant display, do not use the late spring flowering sweet williams, Iceland poppy or stocks. These are best kept to a place by themselves since their flowering season extends into early summer and these will still be appearing when it is time for the summer flowers to go in. To get the best from annuals both hardy and half-hardy it is advisable to keep reasonably close to the suggested sowing times. In common with other plants these have first, a well-defined growing period; flowering time, as a rule, starts when the days are longest, consequently much of the growing stage needs to be completed by then.

2 CULTIVATION
The living soil and how to deal with it

Having decided what and where to plant, now the time comes to discuss the preparation of the site. Most people will already know that soils are largely derived from rocks ground down by the elements. They vary considerably, ranging from the comparatively coarse texture of sand through loam to clay, the smallest of the inorganic constituents. In addition to the finer particles there are also stones and boulders. Known as peat soils, some are almost entirely organic in origin. They frequently have other materials mixed with them to form sandy peat, silty peat and so on. Soil can be described as being a material in which organisms exist, if they do not then it is not soil in the true sense of the word. Although a certain amount of organic breakdown occurs when soils are alternately wet then dry, these organisms (bacteria, worms etc.) are needed to promote final organic decomposition of dead leaves and stems, thus releasing valuable nutrient salts which dissolved in water are taken up by the plants.

A cautionary tale

We once knew a young man whose natural soil was a fertile, rather heavy loam. Although this type of soil produces good crops due to its sticky nature it is difficult to cultivate in wet weather. Somehow the budding gardener discovered that underneath his hard-to-work soil lay a thick band of free-draining yellow sand. The answer he thought was to reverse the order for not only was the sand of a pleasing appearance but it would be easy to rake and cultivate even when damp. We now skip several months during which time a huge excavation has yielded up its sand 'soil' and been refilled with the despised clayey loam. The sand is now spread over flower beds, the kitchen garden and lawn area. Are plants flourishing in the light easily worked but now powder-dry sand? No! Seeds either fail to come up or if they do seldom grow on after germinating, plants remain stunted, even the lawn thin and lifeless. The moral is plain. Improve your existing soil by good cultivation, attention to drainage or moisture retention but never by replacing it with inert material from below. Having said that it must be recognised that this is exactly what happens on a great many new sites not by the owner but rather by the developers' bulldozer. When this happens to you what can be done about it? First try to discover if the existing top-soil has been covered. Covering over rather than removal altogether is in our experience much more common. In this case it is usually possible to double-dig the borders bringing the buried top-soil up from below replacing it with the sub-soil as you dig. The good soil may have a rank smell at first. Do not be concerned about this for it is simply due to the fact that gases from the fermenting weeds have been unable to escape. The smell will soon clear and after a little cultivation the soil should regain its normal fertility once more. Where the top-soil has been removed altogether the only real remedy is to replace it with fresh material purchased for the purpose. Where the sub-soil is not too heavy it may be possible to incorporate into it a certain amount of humus-forming material, peat, compost, spent hops, sawdust etc. cultivating it and eventually turning even that into 'soil'.

Good drainage is an important requirement of cultivated ground. When completely saturated all the spaces in the soil are filled with water instead of air. Consequently the oxygen vital for the functioning of the soil bacteria is no longer present. Badly drained soils have a characteristic dank smell when the ground is dug over. Plant roots rot as parasitic fungi proliferate under these conditions. What can be done to improve drainage? Sharp sand, weathered boiler ash and coarse peat are all useful materials for incorporating in the soil surface. They 'open' the soil which assists in removing much of the water from those borders that are wet in one season and dry in another. Raising the level of these beds will also help with the drainage, although problems could occur when the ground dries out. Where water persists it will be necessary to arrange drains to carry excess moisture away. Simple tile land drains surrounded with stones or ashes leading away from the flower border to a ditch or sump is the traditional way of tackling the job; long lasting pierced plastic pipes are a modern alternative. Failing all else why not create a moisture garden? Some of the finest of all garden flowers flourish under bog conditions.

Gardeners describe their soil as being light, medium or heavy. Generally speaking light soils dry quickly after rain and require the addition of humus-forming materials to retain some of the moisture. Heavy soils on the other hand tend to be wet for long periods then dry out leaving the soil surface cracked and hard. Once again regular applications of organic materials are needed for they act as a conditioner 'opening' the soil making it easier to manage during wet weather and reducing surface cracks when dry. You have only to read old books to learn how essential a part farmyard manure (FYM) formerly played in gardening. It seems that this has now become a scarce commodity. Fortunately, in correctly made garden compost, we have an excellent susbtitute for bulky manure. Please note the words 'correctly made'. So often it seems that confusion arises as to whether a compost heap and the rubbish heap are the same thing. They certainly are not!

Making compost

To many, the bonfire is the most convenient way to dispose of garden refuse. We agree that twigs and woody stems should be burned as well as any obviously diseased plants and roots of perennial weeds. The ash which results from burning plants is a source of potash. It can be spread on bare soils between plants, as soon as it is cool.

All the remaining materials should be rotted down in a compost heap, or container, then later returned to the soil as humus. The compost is actually made by the action of millions of micro-organisms busily engaged in digesting the leaves, grass mowings, chopped plant stems etc. put there for the purpose. Except for cooked food practically any soft organic waste from the kitchen can be used in addition to that from the garden. All we have to do is to provide the correct conditions for the bacteria and insects to operate, and they do the rest. Serious 'organic' gardeners will have at least two compost heaps in different stages of progress; those with a tiny garden may have to make do with a plastic bin. In these the rubbish goes in at the top and if all goes well in a few months compost can be removed from the bottom. The problem of a tiny garden is that insufficient material may accumulate to make the operation worthwhile. If this is your experience why not purchase a bale or two of straw to bulk up the green rubbish? This makes really good compost when correctly rotted down.

Our favourite system for producing regular supplies involves the construction of two or three crates. Made of preserved timber these have removable boards at the front in order to get at the contents when ready. The crates can be made in any size to suit your particular requirements. Incidentally they are bottomless and just sit on the soil in an out-of-the-way spot of the garden. Garden refuse is spread in a 30cm thick layer over the base of the first container followed with a sprinkling of sulphate of ammonia at the rate of 1 tablespoon per square metre. A 5cm layer of sieved garden soil goes on next and is trodden down. After a watering the process is repeated when rubbish is available until the first container is filled. Unless your garden soil is naturally alkaline a dressing of hydrated garden lime over the last layers of sieved soil completes the operation. Make certain that the contents are kept moist by watering every second week or so during dry weather. Should the opposite apply and the rain is making the compost too wet, it is in order to cover the top of the crate with a sheet of polythene. Use the containers in rotation. Good compost takes about six months to make. When the boards which form the front of the container are finally removed the rich, crumbly compost

22

which appears will grow such lovely flowers that any effort needed to make it will be considered worthwhile.

Perfect compost is light and friable, well digested with little smell. In many respects peat, although produced over a considerably longer period, is a similar material. 'Shall I feed it peat? is a familiar question to every nurseryman. The enquirer has obviously been influenced by the copywriter's flair with the free use of such words as rich and dark. Peat really looks good for the soil, and it is. But there is practically no feeding in it. The value lies in its conditioning properties, the ability to open the soil allowing air spaces to be present and also to hold moisture like a sponge during a dry spell. There are two basic types of peat. The finest is that derived from sphagnum moss bogs. It is usually granular, of a light brown colour and comes in tightly compressed bales. This is the peat to use when making your own composts for seed-raising. Sedge peat, on the other hand, is of a finer texture and is suitable for planting and mulching. Always use peat in a moist state for it is almost impossible to dampen it once in the soil. This particularly applies to moss peat. The best way to really wet this kind of peat is to spread the whole bale on a solid concrete area, tread it down then hose it thoroughly. Turn the lot over and repeat the process. Although no-one would consider that peat or compost were as good as FYM for the garden both make a comparable substitute when used in conjunction with an all-round organic fertiliser.

Humus forming materials such as animal or plant manure are most important for the soil because of the physical effect they have on it. In addition, the bacteria present converts the humus into soluble salts which are taken up by roots to build the plant. More concentrated plant 'foods' are the fertilisers both organic in origin and inorganic chemicals. They are used in conjunction with organic manures not in place of them. Many different fertilisers are available ranging from complete formulations down to those for specific purposes. Always sprinkle dry fertilisers carefully on the soil surface, avoiding plant leaves, then lightly hoe in. For quicker results some fertilisers come in a liquid form others are watered or sprayed over the leaves to be absorbed as a foliar feed.

Preparing the ground

Correct cultivation can do much to improve the physical nature of the soil. Just how much work is involved in preparing your soil will depend to a large extent on its composition. Soil texture varies according to the proportions of sand, silt or clay, as well as organic matter present. Where spring planting is to be done, the previous fall will not be too early to make a start toward preparing the site. The ground must be thoroughly dug over using either the garden fork or spade, remove only the largest stones (rocks) as well as all traces of perennial weed roots. The surface may be left rough at this stage since the weather can assist in breaking the soil down into a crumbly tilth or texture. Some gardeners suggest that compost or manure is also spread over the surface at this time. We feel that as most of the nutrients are lost by the leaching action of winter rains the sooner it is dug into the ground the better. If animal manure is fresh, do not allow it to come into contact with the plant roots as the gaseous ammonia present can cause burning. Where possible, complete rough digging of light soils before spring or there is the danger of losing soil moisture due to drying winds and sun.

Planting the border

When the time arrives for planting, first use the garden rake to break the surface of the bed. A light application of a general fertiliser can now be sprinkled onto the soil and gently incorporated. Many annual flowers, although they appreciate feeding, sometimes respond too vigorously if fertiliser is added to the soil at planting time. The result is that they make leaves at the expense of flowers. This can be avoided if the areas where these are to grow are first marked then omitted when the fertiliser is applied. Working from your plan, place a labelled cane in the space each group of plants is to occupy; the bed can be marked with guide lines or, if it is easier, sprinkle a line of contrasting colour sand around the perimeter of each group.

Most plants are supplied in pots these days but if they arrive in trays or flats do not place many in the ground at once for this is a critical time for tender roots, wind or sun both drying them out quickly. Starting with the centre of the bed or border, plant out one sort at a time. A common mistake made by the new gardener is to cram the roots into the planting hole. The procedure for planting is to use the trowel to make the hole rather larger than that required by the plant. Carefully remove the plant from its container or wrapping then place it in the hole with the rootball at a depth slightly deeper than the soil surface. Fill in around the young plant and firm gently using the body's weight above extended fingers to either side of the plant.

Larger open-ground plants should have their roots spread out evenly; any that are spiralling can be straightened. Once again, ensure that the plant is upright, fill in the planting hole and firm gently. If the soil is hard or stony it will be a good practice to have a bucket of prepared potting compost handy to fill in around the roots at this stage. Complete the planting operation by gently watering in each plant individually. Tidy the soil by pricking the surface with your border fork as you continue to plant towards the edge of the bed.

Mulching, watering and weeding

Conservation of soil moisture is a very important part of successful cultivation. This is better than watering itself when possible, for the simple reason that valuable minerals present near the plant roots are not washed away to be lost. There are several materials that may be used for mulching from FYM or compost placed immediately around the plants themselves to a complete ground cover which virtually eliminates weeding too. Here, peat, spent hops from the brewery, shredded tree bark, sawdust or even small stones can be used. Sawdust is one of the cheaper mulches in use. It is far more useful to the plants if it has first been composted for a year using sulphate of ammonia as an activator and regularly watered down. Before applying a mulch of any kind make certain that all weeds that are likely to push through are removed and that the soil is moist. Regular watering, even if not permanently required, will almost certainly be needed during the first season of a new planting. The policy is to ensure that the soil receives a good saturation that almost dries out again before further watering. Frequent light sprinklings during hot weather are worse than useless for this only encourages surface rooting. Keeping plants growing well by incorporating moisture retaining material in the soil prior to planting is the best way of all. Quite apart from competition for available nutrients and moisture, beds or borders are so much more attractive when kept clean and weed-free. In the new planting the bulk of the perennial weeds should have been removed during the initial digging, any which subsequently appear must be dealt with promptly by hand pulling or spot treated with a suitable weedkiller. There are weedkillers available today which can be used prior to planting, others to be used with care among the growing plants. Many gardeners (including ourselves) still prefer the use of hand tools to keep them in check when working in the smaller garden. The hoe must be one of the earliest of tools, its origin lost in obscurity. We own an ancient draw hoe with a broad flat blade. This is a most useful implement and finds frequent use for weed removal, digging, planting holes – even mixing cement at times! On the opposite side is a broad spike. This too is valuable for there is no easier way of breaking up hard lumps of soil than to gradually chop away at them. Modern hoes are normally one of two types. The Dutch, or push hoe, is used by placing the blade on the soil, then as the operator walks slowly backwards he pushes the hoe away from him with short strokes. The draw hoe works in the opposite way. In this case, again taking in a small area at a time, the operator makes small chopping movements as he steps slowly forward. Both tools are excellent for keeping weeds under control and by creating a 'dust mulch' which by presenting a smooth soil surface to the drying elements reduces moisture loss from the ground. Should the inevitable happen and weeds are allowed to develop beyond the small seedling stage, hand pulling may be needed. This will also apply where beds are mulched with a coarse material such as spent hops or sawdust. To most gardeners weeding by hand is not really the irksome task that one would imagine – some will secretly confess that they enjoy doing it! Showery weather is the best time for this kind of weeding for then the soil is soft and weeds come out more easily. Any but those that are seeding make a valuable addition to the compost heap.

Supports

The time to consider staking plants is well before they commence flowering. During their growing stage many of the taller plants will be sturdy and staking will appear to be quite unnecessary. It may well be a different situation by the time their heavy flower spikes are caught by a summer squall. Not all tall plants require staking of course; to find out those which do in your situation may well be a matter of trial and experience. The taller delphiniums are an example of plants which almost invariably require attention in this way. They display their lofty spikes so much better when each is supported with a straight cane. With soft herbaceous plant stems it is most important to make ties not too tight, so as to avoid damage to the green stems. A useful type of support for floppy stemmed plants are 'pea sticks' (in Britain these are often cut from birch, (*Betula pendula*). These can be pushed both in and around each clump of border perennial as they are in their early stages of growth. Admittedly, the beds look awful for a week or two yet before the flowers appear the sticks will be barely visible and the stems held upright in a most natural manner.

Dead heading

Unless seeds are required early flowering plants, such as lupins and delphiniums, will benefit if flowers or flowering stems are removed promptly once they fade. In many instances the result will be a prolonged display as the plant attempts once more to produce seeds in order to maintain the species. From mid-summer remove only the unsightly dead flowers for many plants have dead heads which remain attractive for several weeks.

Further care

Their flowering season over, what then? All annuals and biennnials which have completed their life-cycle should be pulled or dug up and, if no disease appeares to be present, consigned to the compost heap. The space that they occupied can now be lightly forked over or, if conditions permit, thoroughly dug when further planting can follow. From the point of view of perennials it is likely to be preferable to leave them alone until the new growth appears the following spring before their old stems are cut down. Gardeners are tidy people and cut them down to within a few centimetres of the soil before then. There is no set time for this operation. Some plants such as lupins get cut back by simply removing the flower stems as they fade. A second 'flush' of blooms usually follows this prompt action. The cutting down of most border subjects has generally been completed by the time that the last of the lingering fall flowers are over. With the old stems removed, all that there now remains to do in the way of general work is a final weeding and, perhaps, a mulch of compost around the plants as an insurance against winter damage. In warm climates, or if the soil is light, this will also be the season to consider propagation and replanting. Where the soil remains wet, transplanting will be more successful if delayed until the spring. In those countries where moderate to severe frosts occur some additional work regarding winter protection is involved. Here it will be best if the cut stems are replaced over the crowns of the plants, then covered with a layer of compost, leafmould or peat. When spring comes around again any old plant stems that have not rotted down must be removed, exposing the plant crowns once more.

28

3 PROPAGATION
Producing plants at home

It is true to say that one may have a garden bright with flowers without ever sowing a seed or rooting a cutting oneself. Garden centres which stock young plants in season have sprung up wherever there is sufficient demand for them. Here small quantities of bedding-out plants may be purchased at little more than the cost of a few packets of seed. For the average garden this is by far the best method and one which takes much of the guesswork out of planning. Named cultivars of herbaceous perennials and most rock plants are invariably first purchased from a commercial source, either local nursery or specialist grower. New plants can often be produced from these originals later. When it comes to propagating your own plants it will be found that there are two distinct methods depending on whether you are raising short lived subjects such as annuals and biennials, or perennials. Plants in the first group are always raised from seed and although many of the latter can also be increased in this manner they are more often produced vegetatively.

The so-called higher plants (the category into which garden flowers fall) reproduce naturally from seeds in the wild. Although usually imperceptible, seedling variation within the species provides a genetic pool from which only those individuals best suited for survival in a changing environment are left to provide the seeds for the next generation. However, when it comes to garden plants variability in seedlings is not a desired trait. Other factors make garden flowers more variable than their wild ancestors; unless these can be controlled by the seedsman much of the value of a particular cultivar can be lost. For an example, suppose for a moment that you wish to plant up a bed with dwarf antirrhinums. This would not prove to be very successful if some of them turned out to be twice their correct height would it? We should add here that seed can always be used to increase species and botanical varieties. Although they tend to form themselves into a 'breeding line' after several generations seed-raised cultivars of *self*-pollinated annuals will breed true. Consequently they pose few problems for the seedsman who seeks to maintain even stocks. Most species and also cultivars are *cross*-pollinated (although in some cases to complicate things both cross- and self-pollination can occur). When these are raised from seed problems of uniformity will arise due to groups of seedlings being variable. Advantage can be taken of this when new colours appear and the variability maintained. Where the desired colours are selected they are maintained to a standard by growing the stock plants in isolation where accidental further cross-pollination cannot occur.

What are hybrid cultivars?

F_1 hybrids are becoming more common and increasingly popular with discerning growers. The result of repetitive cross-ings, these are the first generation progeny (the F. stands for filial) between two distinct 'lines' each having desired character-istics combined in their offspring. When the parents are selected carefully stock is uniform within the group, in addition most exhibit the phenomenon known as 'hybrid vigour'. The procedure of using two or more parents has to be repeated every time the particular hybrid is required. Although there are exceptions these hybrid plants are seldom used as a seed source as the next (F_2) generation would begin to show signs of variability becoming more uneven in growth and appearance.

Grown naturally, cross-pollinated types could cause problems as there is no control over pollinating insects or wind. The seedgrower overcomes this by selecting identical seed-parents from a single inbred line (not two as in the F_1 hybrids). Stocks of these are then grown on separately from others of the same species. In that way the pollinating agency can only cross-pollinate the identical plants.

Is seed expensive?

We have frequently heard remarks commenting on the high cost of seed. The new gardener might think so having made a purchase, helped in his choice no doubt more by the brightly coloured pictures in the catalogue than anything else. On opening the packet and discovering the often tiny pinch of dust or chaff-like seeds, he may consider that for the amount received it was expensive. From the preceding paragraphs the reader will have gathered that the commercial grower of quality seed has to go to an enormous amount of effort. In the first place he has continually to breed and develop interesting flowers, then having done so build up and maintain stocks to an exacting standard. Flowers are pollinated by insects, wind and also by hand. The methods that the seedsman uses to ensure that the plants are the same as those that appear on the front of the packet are growing seed plants in isolation either by distance or in insect-proof enclosures. In addition, some flowers are cross-pollinated by hand. Where the large-flowered double petunias are concerned this is done by removing the male part of the flower before the anthers shed their pollen. It is usually a nimble-fingered young lady who plays the part of the bee with her fine camel hair brush laden with the pollen from another petunia selected as the parent.

Foil-wrapped seeds

Many seedsmen now use the improved technique of drying the seeds, storing them under strict humidity control until packeting. They are then sealed in foil before being placed in their often brightly coloured outer packets. Once opened the foil inner packet cannot be resealed and therefore all the contents should be sown as soon as practicable. Getting back to the question, is seed expensive? We think not, considering the amount of work involved, although obviously enough high cost of production is reflected in high seed cost.

Gathering seed at home

Seeds of many plants can be saved and either sown at once, or stored then sown at a later date. Raising plants from one's own seeds is at the same time one of the most exciting yet satisfying of all garden pursuits. From the moment of 'birth' these babies are cherished like no others. Choose a fine, dry day for gathering seeds. Cut the stems just as the pods begin to dehice or crack open, forming the stems into small bunches. Enclose the heads in a paper bag, secure the neck of the bag, hang each up by the stems in a warm, airy place. Most of the seeds will fall into the bag and cleaning can be done at a later date. Remember to label them!

How long may flower seeds be kept before sowing?

Viability is measured by the number of seedlings produced from a given number of seeds. The power for seeds to germinate varies with the species. Most start degenerating after five years storage and would not really be worth sowing after ten. Some, such as Primula, Meconopsis and Delphinium should be sown as soon as ripe. Annual aster (*Callistephus* sp.) are also in the short lived group. These must be sown before two seasons have elapsed. In most cases it is better to sow seed as soon as purchased.

Raising flowers from seed

For simplicity it is usual to divide seed-raised plants into three groups
1   Half hardy annuals
2   Hardy annuals
3   Biennals and perennials

Half hardy annuals

As their name suggests these are frost tender plants requiring the protection of a heated greenhouse or frame in their early seedling stages. Consequently these are not planted out until all danger from frost is past. In practice it will also be found that plants of the other two groups may be raised in a similar manner. That is to say they are grown in seed trays (flats) under cover for later planting. The reason being that, although hardy, indoor seedling production provides far better germination and growth control than is available outside.

Hardy annuals

These are usually sown directly in the ground where they are to flower.

Biennials and perennials

These can be either sown in rows in a sheltered position, outside, or in a greenhouse to start them off. The next step is to transplant them to nursery rows before being finally placed in their flowering positions. Biennials always flower in their second year. Perennials frequently flower in their second growing season but may take a further year or longer to reach flowering size.

Composts and cleanliness

Sterilised seed sowing compost can normally be purchased from a horticultural retailer or garden centre. It differs from the more familiar potting composts in that it is both finer in texture and contains less fertiliser. Most seedlings can be grown in the same formulation until planted out. Alternatively a suitable seed raising compost can be made up at home combining 2 parts of loam (sterilised) passed through a fine sieve; 1 part moist peat (fine or medium grade sphagnum for preference); 1 part clean sharp sand. To each bushel (about 36 litres) add 56g (2oz) ground limestone (chalk) and 56g (2oz) superphosphate of lime. Turn the materials completely three times then store under cover. If at all possible leave for two to three days before using. Cleanliness is the rule in propagation. Sterile compost is imperative. Seed trays must be scrubbed clean if not new then dried in the sun before use. If it is available, treated seed is to be preferred. The dangers at this stage are pre-emergence, damping off then post-emergence stem rot. Later when the plants are older rootlets can be attacked by injurious fungi. Known as root rot this and the other problems mentioned can be almost eliminated by good sanitation in general. In addition the environmental conditions are present during germination. These can affect both the growth rate of the plants and that of attacking fungi. Seedlings of species which require high temperatures are particularly susceptible if the soil and air temperatures fall too low. It is also true to say that the correct moisture content of the compost is important too. Overwatering is the usual mistake although in high air temperatures with dry compost underwatering is just as bad. Poor drainage of the seed boxes and lack of ventilation (high humidity) for the young plants can also cause failures.

Seeds

When all is ready the exciting process of seed sowing can begin. We use the word exciting for who since childhood has not looked forward with eager anticipation first of all to the emergence of tiny leaves, next the plant and finally the flower? Surely, little gives more pleasure than seeing a bed of flowers which a few short weeks before were nothing more than a packet of dry dust-like particles. A living miracle which all can witness is something that is repeated millions of times both in the wild and in gardens each season.

How to sow

Seed trays are first of all loosely filled with seed sowing compost, then to ensure an even surface firmed using a small board. A light watering settles the material. After allowing a short period for the trays to drain the seeds may be sown. Even distribution of small seed is important and made easier if it is first of all mixed with a little fine dry sand. The seed/sand mixture is sprinkled together over the whole surface. The sowing operation is completed by shaking a little compost over the seeds. We use a fine wire seive 'borrowed' from the kitchen for this. The depth of the covering depends largely on the size of the seeds, small seeds requiring very little. Some of the larger seeds, such as those of the sweet pea, need either soaking in water overnight or chipping before they are sown for the seedcoat of many of the large seeds is very hard indeed. After sowing the boxes are labelled with the name of the plant and the date – something that may prove very useful for future records. A pane of glass covered with a sheet of brown paper is next placed over the box. The paper must be thick enough to exclude most of the light. Turn and wipe the glass occasionally. Very little, if any, watering will be needed until the seedlings of most plants appear. If a greenhouse is being used for germinating the seeds the boxes can be put out of the way under the benches. We always scatter a few slug pellets around. They deal with those unwelcome pests whose favourite meal consists of boxes of germinating seeds.

Plant growth is controlled by day/night length. In the germination of most of the species commonly encountered, moisture plus fluctuating day/night temperatures triggers growth into action. The initial expansion of the seed as it absorbs water is mechanical (housewives will know how dried beans, peas etc. swell after soaking). The next stage in the germinating flower seed is sufficient warmth; prolonged low day temperatures inhibits growth which frequently causes damage to the emerging root and bud. For even germination an average day temperature of 15°C should be the aim.

Pricking out

As soon as the seed leaves appear the paper covering must be removed and the boxes placed on the glasshouse staging where they receive the maximum light. The sheet of glass can be tilted at one end in order to allow the free circulation of air over the seedlings. This can be removed altogether within a few days.

When the plantlets are showing their first true leaves is the usual time for transplanting. A similar compost to that used for the initial sowing will be satisfactory for the smaller growing plants. The more vigorous kinds such as dahlias can be pricked out into boxes or small pots filled with a compost containing a lean fertiliser formulation. Once more the boxes are filled, firmed, lightly watered and left to drain. Each tiny seedling is gently picked by one 'ear' (you will understand what this means when your seedlings appear), and dibbled in with a pencil or sharpened stick. Commercial producers tend to cram too many seedlings into a box. Far better plants result – sturdier with plenty of roots – if plenty of space is allowed for each. Why not try say 30 to a box (5 × 6 rows)? Add the date of pricking out to your original label if you wish to keep a record of this. A careful watering with the finest rose on the can completes the pricking-out operation. If this is done in hot weather place the complete trays of tiny transplants in a shaded place out of the direct rays of the sun for a few days as a precaution against wilting. Once they have recovered from their move a light airy place is best for them. Although most annuals eventually branch naturally others are not as willing to do this. We can encourage these by simply nipping out their growing tips between finger and thumb. Many kinds respond by becoming well-branched instead of 'leggy'. Kinds to pinch out include *Antirrhinum*, *Phlox*, *Salpiglossis* etc. Others such as *Cleome*, *Tagetes* and *Zinnia* will not require this treatment.

Hardening off

The hardening off process varies with the climate of the particular locality. Suffice it to say that plants must not be allowed to suffer frost damage. When first removed from their sheltered environment even normally hardy plants can be severely burned if the transfer takes place suddenly. The greenhouse of most amateur growers contains such a variety of plants in so many different stages of growth that reducing the temperature and admitting more air via the ventilators is not feasible. Here the unheated garden frame comes into its own. Because it is much lower the boxes of seedlings can be placed near the light. In the frame, ventilate on sunny days then close up at night. If frost is forecast, mats or sacking placed over the glass will keep out the cold. Eventually, prior to planting out, the glass may be left off altogether.

In warmer countries where late frost is no hazard hot sun burning down on the small seedlings would be the danger. Here the shade house can replace the garden frame for the hardening off operation.

Window gardens

These days many people do not possess a garden in the accepted sense yet wish to produce flowers (and vegetables, too, for that matter) for their balcony, flat or home unit garden. The general methods described above for raising seedlings at home can be scaled down to suit the smaller requirements. Instead of seed trays, flowers pots are used, plastic domes or even polythene bags with wire supports instead of a greenhouse. Window glass transmits considerable heat which is likely to burn tender seedlings very quickly. After germinating your seeds in a dark place transfer the pots to an inside window ledge that seldom receives the full glare of the sun. The tiny plants will grow toward the light; you can correct their leaning habit by giving the pots a half turn each day.

Biennials and perennials

Biennials which are used in bedding schemes or planted out in borders are always grown from seed. Apart from the many named cultivars, border perennials and rockery plants can be raised this way too.

In addition to the better environmental control obtained in initial sowing in a greenhouse both these groups of plants may be raised out of doors. This takes place in a well prepared, friable, adequately drained site. Do you have a space where a winter or early crop has been taken off? If the surface of the soil can be broken down into a fine tilth suitable for tiny seedlings this would be ideal. The tendency always seems to be for late sowing. We consider that for most subjects this is a mistake. The first season sees biennials growing into big leafy plants ready for transplanting in the fall. Their next year is taken up with flowering.

When preparing the soil for sowing seeds out of doors, first rake the soil to provide a fine crumbly surface. Seeds are sown in drills. A drill is a shallow depression made by drawing the tip of a hoe along one side of a tightly stretched garden line. After a light covering, the soil over the seeds should be firmed by treading or tapping down with the back of a spade. A gentle watering should start the germination process. It is very important either to sow the seeds very thinly, or thin the plantlets later, for these have to be sturdy specimens each with a well-formed root system. Some gardeners get good results by sowing seeds normally then transplanting all the seedlings when large enough to handle. Perennials are often grown on in a nursery bed for one or two seasons before being planted out in their flowering positions.

How perennials are increased

Many border plants such as lupins, delphiniums etc. are raised from seed. They develop into good specimens with interesting colours. There is a drawback however for, except for the species that are grown, most present-day garden perennials are named cultivars. Derived initially from a single individual they are distinct from other named kinds by reason of colour, form, height etc. These named cultivars are increased and maintained

38

artificially by vegetative means only. These are: division of roots, either when dormant or just starting into growth; cuttings of stem or root and, lastly, grafting – an art which is outside the scope of the home gardener. The great advantage in these methods of propagation is the fact that unlike seedlings the identical characteristics of the parent are faithfully reproduced each time, that being so it is possible to build up an even stock quickly.

Cuttings

Green shoot cuttings can be made from the majority of herbaceous and rockery plants. The young stems as they appear in the spring are suitable material for border plants; side shoots taken in the summer months after flowering are generally speaking better for rockery subjects.

Bottomless box method of rooting cuttings

As the new shoots selected for cuttings are very soft when taken, they wilt easily, and would more often than not die if put straight into the soil. One structure which maintains humidity, allowing the cutting to remain turgid as it is recovering from the shock of its removal, is a roughly constructed rooting box. This is simply a four-sided bottomless box set into the soil almost to its rim. The size of the frame can vary according to the materials available. A suitable size to start with could be quite small say 60 × 45cm (24in × 18in). The timber needs to be at least 23cm (9in) deep. Excavate the soil where the frame is to sit and when in place half-fill it with a mixture of 1 part sand or pumice to 1 part of peat or leafmould. A pane of clear glass is now put in place and after watering well the cutting box is ready for use. Most herbaceous plants have hollow stems. For this reason it is best to prepare your cuttings with a 'heel' or portion of the original rootstock. This is trimmed carefully and the lower leaves removed before inserting the cuttings. Alternatively they can be cut first below a node or leaf joint. Select firm stocky shoots approx. 10cm (4in) in length of most subjects, rock plants and other small growers will be shorter than this. Later, with a small trowel, lift the rooted plants carefully leaving as much compost as possible adhering to them. These youngsters are normally planted straight out where they are to remain. In the old days bell-glasses were used as an aid to rooting cuttings out of doors. A plastic bag over a wire frame could be regarded as a modern substitute. These are also used for a day or so to prevent wilting until the new plant can fend for itself.

Are rooting hormones required?

Plant hormones are complex organic compounds produced by the plant. These materials move within the plant to regulate its physiological processes such as the initiation of buds, stem length and also rooting. Commercially produced rooting hormones are synthetic compounds which when applied to the base of the cutting assist the natural hormones already present in the production of roots. In addition, some of these formulations include a fungicide to fight the ever present invading organisms. (Given the correct environmental conditions those herbaceous plants normally raised from cuttings root readily. Having said this we feel that anything which can assist in the production of new plants must be considered an advantage.) Usually marketed in the form of a powder, the base of the cutting is first dipped in water and then in the powder. Excess powder is shaken off before inserting the cutting in the rooting medium. The lowest strength material may prove useful for 'difficult' subjects although few herbaceous plants which are normally increased from cuttings really come into this category.

Division

Where most kinds of border subjects are concerned the division of the roots when the plant is dormant, or just starting into growth, is at the same time one of the easier means of propagation, and also essential for the general well-being of the plants. When they have been growing well for several seasons they tend to lose vigour due to the fact that a mass of tangled roots has developed. Dead or decaying growth may be crammed into their centres with new shoots pushing through only at the edges of the plant. The tried and trusted method of dealing with such a specimen is to divide it up, discarding all worn out parts and replanting in fresh soil only the young vigorous portions. Before they swamp their neighbours some of the rampant growers require similar treatment. Keeping each clump young and vigorous means more flowers of better quality. It is surprising just how tough and woody the centres of some plants can become in just a few seasons of growth. No amount of tugging or pulling can coax the roots apart. Gardeners discovered years ago that by first lifting the plant and inserting two border forks back to back in the centre of the clumps they could lever them apart with less damage to the roots than simply hacking them apart with a spade. Single crowns of certain plants such as the Michaelmas daisies (*Aster* sp) and various kinds of chrysanthemum can be detached after the parents have flowered. Dibbled into a cold frame for the winter months these make up into fine sturdy specimens as they grow away after planting out the following spring.

Root cuttings

Although a great many of the hardy herbaceous plants can be split up into separate crowns there are others, including most of those with deep prong-like roots, which not only resent disturbance but if dug up cannot be divided in the normal manner. Many of these can be increased by means of root cuttings. Pieces of dormant root are removed from the lifted plant, cut into sections and placed upright in pots, boxes or the open ground depending on species. Ensure that the pieces of root are inserted the correct way up and do not use rooting hormone on these as bud inhibition will most likely occur. Some species form new buds quickly, these grow away strongly soon after preparation, others develop an extensive root system before their top growth appears. When the operation is started in the winter most plants grown from root cuttings will be large enough to place in their permanent positions by late spring. More details of plants suitable for propagation from root cuttings will be found under their respective headings.

4 THE GARDENER'S ENEMIES

Insects are present in every garden for they are part of the living natural world that surrounds us. The gardener's aim should not be to banish all insect life from the garden but to acheive some measure of control over them. The troubles that *could* affect plants are legion. These include chewing or sucking insects, moulds or rusts. They are ever present ready to take their toll. It is not that an attack on garden flowers would herald an economic disaster but we do not care to see our treasures damaged or destroyed for want of a little forethought. It seems just a few short years ago that the remedies available for insect or fungus attack could be counted on one hand. Some were applied with watering can or sprayer, others dusted on by means of a muslin bag or applied by lighting a pile of nicotine shreds. These days the garden centre shelves are stacked high with (mostly) complex chemicals in varied brands. These are sold as aerosols, puffer cartons, bottles of concentrate, packets of powder and so on. Used correctly there is no doubt that the modern methods of control are safer (to the operator) although, as they tend to be more specific in their use, choosing the correct formulation is not always easy. In almost all cases it is best to take action when needed rather than spray indiscriminately. Over-use could also destroy the pests' natural predators. The materials selected must be varied in use for there is a real danger that resistant strains of insects could build up unless this is done. Some of the newer chemicals are termed persistent which means that their effectiveness is longer lasting than earlier formulations. Others are systemic which are absorbed through the tissues and into the sapstream of the plant. The pests are subsequently poisoned through the plant rather than by wetting their bodies, which has the effect of cutting off their air supply or affecting their nervous systems.

All parts of plants can be affected by disorders. Roots may rot or get eaten by soil insects. Stems are bored, leaves holed or the sap sucked, even flowers disfigured. Only by diagnosing the problem can we remedy it. That is why it is important to learn how to identify pests and diseases. The next step is find the most suitable antidote. Pesticides are applied as aerosols, dusts or granules and sprays. Aerosols are often formulated with more than one chemical in order to give a wider range of use. They are ready-mixed in the correct proportions, pressurised so that all the operator has to do is to hold the can near the plant and press the button. There are some dangers with this method of application – flower damage, leaf scorch etc. – but these can be mostly avoided by adhering to the manufacturer's instructions. The biggest drawback with aerosols must be their cost. Perhaps they are suitable if you have a tiny patio garden but with anything larger they could prove very expensive. On the subject of economics, dusts are also costly for the home gardener simply because without efficient powered blowers they are difficult to apply. Hand application can easily spoil the appearance of the plants. This is not to say that they do not have their uses: on ant runs, as soil insecticides and so on. For the latter purpose the recently marketed granules are very useful and are easy to apply when shaken from their special pack. Mixing the powder or liquid formulation with water and applying the spray as a mist is by far the best method of combating garden troubles. With the introduction of relatively inexpensive plastic hand sprayers this system is both economic and efficient in almost all cases. Several chemicals are compatible which means that two or more materials can be mixed in order to combat widely differing disorders, such as insects and a fungus disease, at the same time. Correct measurement of materials is of the utmost importance. Too little means that the spray is ineffective, but if too concentrated damage of the plants is likely. Thorough wetting of all leaf surfaces, stems and buds is important for if pests are missed the chances are that the infestation will continue unabated. The exception could be when using systemic materials

44

some of which are sprayed on to the soil and which are absorbed into the plant. The stages at which garden pests (we include insects, red spiders, mites, woodlice, millepedes) are at their most injurious depends on the pest and to a lesser extent on the plant victim. Some butterflies and moths bite portions from the roots or leaves at the larval stage which is the only time they injure plants. When adult, their feeding is confined to nectar-sucking. The large group of aphides (greenflies and other plant lice) are equipped with needle-like mouth-parts with which to suck the sap by piercing the cells. These are active throughout their lives as are many of the beetles and weevils, where the damage by larvae on the roots is almost matched by that of the adult on the leaves.

The best time to spray is in the late afternoon or cool of the evening for then the chances of killing bees, which work among the flowers, butterflies and useful insects, is lessened. Also keep the spray away from flowers for they are easily marked and ruined. Most modern persistent materials are extremely toxic to fish so this is another area in which care must be taken. Do not spray when it is windy for there is a danger of spray drifting over food crops ready for harvesting. Check the spray pattern on the foliage to see that the droplets cling, not so fine that it drifts away as a fine mist or too heavy so that it runs off the leaf edges easily. Spraying should be done at the first sign of an attack and if necessary followed up with repeat spraying, for in many cases only the active stages of the pest are affected, and eggs continue to hatch which provide subsequent generations. Unlike greenhouse plants, roses, fuchsias, chrysanthemums etc. it is by no means essential to adopt a regular spraying programme for garden flowers. For one thing it would be a waste of spray material and another could quite easily destroy predatory insects actually in the process of keeping your pests under control for you! So much for insect pests where spraying is a cure. Where fungus diseases are involved the aim is to prevent an attack. This has to be anticipated and is generally worse under humid conditions. In addition remedial spraying can normally halt the spread of a disease.

Care of materials and safety

As well as being lethal to insects, modern materials are, in sufficient quantities, lethal to humans too. That is why in commercial establishments they are (and, if not, should be) kept in a locked cupboard marked 'Poisons'. The amateur gardener must ensure that all dilute sprays are used on the day that they are mixed. Concentrated packs must be stored high up, well out of the reach of children or pets, and when empty disposed of sensibly. Unless tiny amounts are involved we prefer to wear overalls when working with the sprayer in our garden. Plastic gloves should always be worn both when filling the sprayer and during use. Do not breathe the spray mist or allow it to fall on exposed skin. In any case a thorough wash with soap and warm water should always be had immediately on completion of the work.

Check list of plant pests and disorders and their remedies

Note : the names of suggested remedies are those of the chemicals used in their formulation. Trade brand names will almost certainly differ from country to country. It should however be possible to identify most of these by the contents on the pack.

LEAVES – Insects Visible
Aphid
Identification   Colonies of small round-bodied black- or green-fly clustered on young shoots and leaves. They cause damage by sucking the sap.

Active period   Spring, summer.

Plants affected   Most when making soft growth.

Remedy   Clear the area of all weeds some of which can harbour these pests. Spray: dimethoate, formothion, menazon, derris, lindane, malathion, pirimicarb, pyrethrum.

Whitefly
Identification   Groups of tiny white moth-like insects together with their green scale-like stage under leaves.
Active period   Hot weather only, outside.
Plants affected   Many including chrysanthemum, zinnia etc.
Remedy   Spray: diazinon, malathion, pyrethrum.

LEAVES – Other Damage
Caterpillars
Identification   Holes eaten in leaves by pest (often present); Leaves held together by web (insect present).
Active period   Growing season.
Plants affected   Most.
Remedy   Remove any pests visible and destroy. Spray or dust: carbaryl, derris, lindane, malathion, pirimiophos.

Capsid bug
Identification   Small ragged holes in young leaves caused by bright green sucking insects.
Active period   Spring, summer.
Plants affected   Some including chrysanthemum and dahlia.
Remedy   Spray: fenitrothion, lindane, malathion.

Earwig
Identification   Small holes in leaves caused by insects active at night.
Active period   Growing season.
Plants affected   Some including dahlia, chrysanthemum.
Remedy   Remove dead leaves from the base of stems, remove rubbish from vicinity. Spray or dust: diazinon, lindane, triclorphon.

Flea beetle
Identification   Leaves peppered with small holes; black metallic jumping insects seen when the leaves are disturbed.

Active period   Spring.
Plants affected   Aubrieta, wallflower and other crucifers.
Remedy   Clear area of weeds – particularly members of the Cruciferae. Keep plants growing well during dry spring weather. Dust: carbaryl, derris, diazinon.

Froghopper
Identification   Plants disfigured by mass of 'cuckoo-spit'.
Active period   Spring and early summer.
Plants affected   Many.
Remedy   Hose plants to remove 'spit'. Spray: lindane, malathion.

Fusarium wilt
Identification   Leaves discoloured, stems wilt due to presence of parasitic fungi.
Active period   Growing season.
Plants affected   *Dianthus* sp, Sweet pea.
Remedy   Burn infected plants, replant healthy material elsewhere.

Leaf-hopper
Identification   Areas of scraped tissue on leaves caused by the adults of froghopper insects.
Active period   Growing season.
Plants affected   Some including chrysanthemum, *Primula*, pelargonium.
Remedy   Remove all weeds from the garden area so as to reduce places for breeding and over-wintering adults. Spray: carbaryl, diazinon, formothion, lindane, nicotine, pyrethrum.

Leaf miner
Identification   Twisting white lines between the upper and lower skins of the leaf caused by the larvae of various species of fly (*Diptera*).
Active period   Growing season.

Plants affected   Several including: chrysanthemum, *Tagetes* etc.

Remedy   Clear weeds from area to remove host plants; pick off mined leaves or squeeze to kill larvae. Apply stimulant to plant in order for it to recover vigour. Spray: diazinon, lindane, malathion.

Red spider mite

Identification   Leaves dry and mottled by sap-sucking mites beneath, lower leaves finely webbed (normally a glasshouse pest but can occur outside).

Active period   Summer, autumn during hot, dry weather.

Plants affected   Many.

Remedy   Well space plant, maintain humid atmosphere by watering over and around affected plants. Spray: derris, dimethoate, malathion. (Difficult to control)

Slugs and snails

Identification   Large or small portions of leaves eaten – seedlings frequently completely by these large slow moving insects.

Active period   Growing period in damp humid weather.

Plants affected   All seedlings delphiniums, sweet pea, primula.

Remedy   Remove surface litter and other hiding places. Use slug baits methiocarb, metaldehyde.

Thrips

Identification   Leaves mottled silvery on stunted or dis-figured shoots by narrow sucking insects which scrape the plants' surface tissues.

Active period   Summer, autumn.

Plants affected   Some border and rock plants.

Remedy   Spray: carbaryl, derris, diazinon, dimethoate, lindane, malathion, pyrethrum.

Virus (various)

Identification   Leaves wrinkled and distorted, flowers often distorted.
Active period   Growing season.
Plants affected   Many.
Remedy   No cure, burn affected plants. Replant fresh stock elsewhere.

Weevil
Identification   Holes in leaves caused by small night feeding beetles.
Active period   Growing season.
Plants affected   Some including *Primula* sp.
Remedy   Spray: carbaryl, diazinon, pirimiphos, methyl.

LEAVES – Fungus Visible
Botrytis (Grey mould)
Identification   Grey patches on leaves and rotting stems caused by fungus.
Active period   Summer, autumn in dull wet weather.
Plants affected   Some including clarkia, chrysanthemum and zinnia.
Remedy   Cut away infected leaves and stems, burn. Dust with captan. Spray: benomyl, thiram, zineb.

Powdery mildew
Identification   White mealy mould covers leaves and flowers due to presence of parasitic fungus.
Active period   Growing season more prevalent in autumn.
Plants affected   Many include *Aster* sp. calendula, antirrhinum etc.
Remedy   Remove badly infected shoots, prune or thin shoots where possible in order to promote free circulation of air. Spray: (10–14 day intervals as a preventative) benomyl, dinocap.

50

Rust(s)
Identification   Rust-like orange or yellow patches caused by parasitic fungus on foliage and flowers.
Active period   Growing season (Sweet William – autumn).
Plants affected   Hollyhock, Sweet William, antirrhinum.
Remedy   Spray: (preventative not cure) maneb, thiram, zineb.

SHOOTS – Distorted, Wilted or Dead
Aster wilt
Identification   Plant grows well then collapses.
Active period   Summer.
Plants affected   China asters.
Remedy   Burn infected stock. Rotate planting positions.

Rhizome rot
Identification   Rhizomes rot at growing point at base of leaves.
Active period   All year during wet weather.
Plants affected   *Iris* sp. (large-flowered iris).
Remedy   Cut away infected portions and burn; improve drainage. Dust cut surfaces with captan.

Sclerotinia rot
Identification   Stems covered with woolly white mould.
Active period   Spring summer.
Plants affected   Some including dahlia.
Remedy   Cut away infected parts and burn. Dust with captan.

Verticillium wilt
Identification   Stems wilt and eventually die.
Active period   Growing season.
Plants affected   *Aster* sp.
Remedy   Burn diseased stock. Rotate planting position.

ROOTS DAMAGED – Poor Growth
Cabbage root fly
Identification   Plants stunted, seedlings collapse due to roots being eaten. Small white maggots present.
Active period   Growing season.
Plants affected   Wallflower, stock and other Cruciferae.
Remedy   Lift affected plants with ball of soil and burn. Water remaining plants with spray strength bromophos, diazinon, lindane.

Chafer grub
Identification   Plants stunted due to roots being eaten. Fat white grub of beetle usually present.
Active period   Spring, summer.
Plants affected   Most including all seedlings.
Remedy   Apply soil dressing granules when cultivating former grassland bromophos, diazinon.

Chrysanthemum stool miner
Identification   Roots eaten, maggots of fly bore into stools causing damage so that cuttings are unobtainable.
Active period   Autumn, winter, spring.
Plants affected   Chrysanthemum.
Remedy   Dust or spray with derris, lindane, malathion.

Club root
Identification   Poor growth, leaves yellow, roots swollen due to attack by parasitic fungus.
Active period   Growing season.
Plants affected   Some including stock, wallflower.
Remedy   Apply lime or ground chalk to acid soils.

Cutworm
Identification   Seedlings collapse after being eaten through at ground level, caterpillar sometimes present.
Active period   Spring, autumn.

Plants affected   Most seedlings.
Remedy   Dust or spray: bromophos, diazinon, triclorphon.

Leatherjacket (larvae of crane-fly)
Identification   Poor growth of individuals, seedlings collapse due to roots being eaten, caterpillar present.
Active period   Spring, summer.
Plants affected   Most, including all seedlings.
Remedy   Good cultivation and drainage to discourage the attentions of adult winged flies. Soil dressing: carbaryl, diazinon, methiocarb.

Millepede
Identification   Seedling roots eaten, dark cylindrical many-legged pests also present to extend damage caused by slugs and snails.
Active period   Growing season (also in stored dahlia roots).
Plants affected   Most including all seedlings.
Remedy   Dust or spray: carbaryl, diazinon, pirimiphos methyl.

Root aphis
Identification   Poor growth of individuals, dark grey insects clustered on roots.
Active period   Summer, autumn.
Plants affected   Most.
Remedy   Water with spray strength solution: malathion, diazinon, nicotine.

Weevil
Identification   Poor growth or sudden collapse due to roots being eaten by weevil larvae (present among roots of carefully lifted plants).
Active period   Summer, autumn.
Plants affected •   Most.
Remedy   Water with a spray strength solution: malathion,

53

diazinon, nicotine.

Wireworm
Identification   Poor growth of individuals, seedlings collapse as roots are eaten, yellow grub present.
Active period   Spring, summer.
Plants affected   Many including all seedlings.
Remedy   Soil dressing: bromophos, diazinon.

Woodlouse
Identification   Roots, stems eaten. Damage difficult to attribute is often caused by this pest.
Active period   Growing season. Winter in stored dahlia tubers.
Plants affected   Many including *Primula* sp. alpines and shade-loving plants.
Remedy   Dust or spray: bromophos, diazinon.

FLOWER DAMAGE
Caterpillar
Identification   Petals eaten, pest present.
Active period   When flowering.
Plants affected   Few including chrysanthemum.
Remedy   Pick off caterpillars.

Earwig
Identification   Holes eaten in petals, insects present.
Active period   When flowering.
Plants affected   Few including dahlia and chrysanthemum.
Remedy   Trap insects in flower pots stuffed with straw.

Petal Blight
Identification   Dark spots on petals which rot away.
Active period   When flowering.
Plants affected   Some including chrysanthemum.
Remedy   Destroy infected bloom, spray unopened buds with zineb.

THE COLOUR PLATES

1   Moisture loving plants *Astilbe* 'Cologne' (front); *Primula* florindae (rear).

2 *Anthemis cupaniana.*

3 Rock plants, *Aethionema ;* thrift and saxifrage.

4   *Aster alpinus.*

5   *Aster amellus* 'King George'.

6   Acrolinium (*Helipterum roseum*)

7 *Alchemilla mollis.*

8 *Acanthus spinosus.*

10 Snapdragons, *Antirrhinum majus* cvs.

9 *Anchusa azurea* 'Royal Blue'.

11 Rock plants, *Armeria maritima* 'Alba' (left); rock phlox (right).

12 *Armeria caespitosa.*

13 *Aubrieta deltoidea* 'Red Carpet'.

14　*Aster thompsonii* 'Nana'.

15　*Ageratum* 'Biscay'.　　　　16　*Anagallis monelli.*

17 *Brachycombe iberidifolia.*

18 *Begonia semperflorens.*

19 *Antirrhinum* 'Hummingbird' mixed, with *Tagetes signata* in the background.

20 *Canna* or Indian Shot in a New Zealand garden.

21 *Callistephus chinensis* 'Teisa Stars'.

22 *Calceolaria* 'Sunshine'.

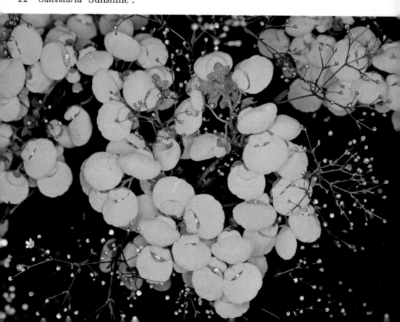

23 *Celosia argentea* Plumosa
    'Fairy Fountains'.

24 Candytuft, (*Iberis umbellata*)
    'Dwarf Fairy' mixed.

25 *Callistephus chinensis*, mixed.

26 *Callistephus* or China asters.

27   Chrysanthemum 'Mabel'.

28 *Campanula persicifolia.*

29 *Campanula lactiflora* 'Loddon Anna'.

30 *Coreopsis verticillata* 'Grandiflora'.

31   *Chrysanthemum multicaule* 'Gold Plate'.

32   *Campanula turbinata.*

33 *Catananche caerulea.*

34 Cosmea, *(Cosmos bipinnatus).*

35   Chrysanthemum 'Fairie'.

36   Chrys. 'Piccolino'.

37   Chrys. 'Solley'.

38   Chrys. 'Salmon Fairie'.

39   Chrys. 'Pamela'.   40   Chrys. 'Grandchild'.

41   *Chrysanthemum maximum* 'Wirral Supreme'.

42 Chrysanthemum 'Heide'.

43 Chrys. 'Bellair'.

44 Chrys. 'Pinxton'.

46 Chrys. 'Crimson Yvonne Arnaud'.

45 Chrys. 'Elvin'.

47 *Cleome spinosa* 'Rose Queen'.

48　Dahlia 'Kathy'.

49　Dahlia 'Laura Eileen'.

50　Dahlia 'Hamari Katrina'.

51　Dahlia 'Freda Crosby'.

52 Dahlia 'Lavengro'.

53 Dahlia 'John Street'.

54 Dahlia 'Nijinksky'.

55 Dahlia 'Quel Diable'.

56 Dahlia 'Chimborazo'.

57   Annual delphinium or Larkspur 'Dwarf Rocket.'

58   Larkspur, fine for cutting.   59   *Digitalis purpurea* 'Excelsior'.

60   Delphinium 'Pacific Hybrids'.

61 Del. 'Butterball'.

62 Del. 'Summer Wine'.

63 Del. 'Royal Marine'.

64 Del. 'Shimmer'.

65 *Dimorphotheca aurantiaca* 'Salmon Dwarf'.

66 *Echium* 'Blue Bedder'; *Dimorphotheca* 'Giant Orange' (left).

67 *Dianthus barbatus* (Sweet William).

68 Dimorphotheca, 'African Beauty'.

69 *Dianthus* 'White Charm'.

70 D. 'Whitehills'.

71 D. (Carnation) 'Dwarf
Vienna'.

72 D. 'Brilliancy'.

73   *Eschscholzia californica* 'Monarch Art Shades'.

74   *Erigeron macranthus*.

75 *Echinacea purpurea* 'The King'.

76 *Eryngium alpinum.*

77   *Cynara cardunculus.*

78   Globe thistles with Meadow Rue (rear).

79   Clarkia, Double mixed.

80 *Filipendula purpurea.*

81 *Gentiana septemfida.*

82 *Gypsophila repens* 'Dorothy Teacher'.

83 *Geranium cinereum.*

84 *G.* 'Ballerina'.

85 *Godetia* 'Sybil Sherwood'.

86 *Helenium autumnale*
'Moerheim Beauty'.

87 *Helichr̄ysum bracteatum* 'Hot
Bikini'.

88 *Helleborus lividus* var. *corsicus*.

89   *Hutchinsia alpina.*

90   *Heliopsis scabra* 'Ballet Dancer'.

91 *Jasione perennis.*

92 *Hemerocallis* 'Stafford'.

93 *Helianthus* 'Sungold' (right);
    Amaranthus caudatus (rear).

94-97   Some modern large-flowered Iris cvs.

98 *Kniphofia* 'Winter Cheer'.

99 *Kniphofia* 'Modesta'.

101 *Ligularia stenocephala* 'The Rocket'.

100 *Inula royleana*

102   Sweet pea, (*Lathyrus odoratus*) 'Jet Set'.

103   Leptosiphon, *Gilia hybrida*.

104   *Lavatera trimestris* 'Tanagra'

105 *Lythrum virgatum* 'The Rocket'.

106 *Lupinus* (annual) 'Pixie' strain.

107 Marigold, *Calendula officinalis* 'Art Shades'.

108 *Meconopsis* × *sheldonii*

109 *Myosotidium hortensia.*

110 Plants for part shade, *Primula* and *Meconopsis.*

111 *Mesembryanthemum criniflorum.*

112 *Monarda didyma*
'Cambridge Scarlet'.

113 *Mimulus* × *burnetii.*

114 *Galega officinalis* 'Hartlandii'.

115 *Malva alcea* 'Fastigiata'.

116 Colour contrast, *Monarda* (red) and *Dracocephalum*.

117 *Phacelia campanularia.*

118 Poppy, *Papaver rhoeas*
     'Ladybird'.

119 *Nasturtium* 'Red Roulette'.

120 *Matricaria eximia* 'Golden
     Ball'.

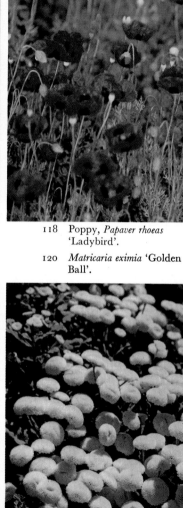

121 *Nicotiana* 'Crimson Rock' with a 'dot' plant of *Ricinus*.

122 *Paeonia officinalis* 'Rubra Plena'.

123 *Onosma albo-roseum.*

124 *Paeonia* 'William Cranfield'.

125 *Salvia sclarea.*

126 *Rudbeckia* 'Herbstsonne'.

128 Opium poppies and cornflowers.

127 *Lychnis chalcedonica.*

129   Regal pelargonium 'Circus Days'.

130   Marigold 'Red Brocade'.

131   Petunias and lobelia brighten a windowbox all summer.

132   Ivy-leaved geranium, fine
      for hanging baskets.

133   *Portulaca grandiflora*,
      Double mixed.

134   Border phlox 'Hampton Court' with *Penstemon* 'Evelyn'.

135   *Phlox* 'Crackerjack'.

136   *Phlox subulata* 'Alexander's Surprise'.

137 *Nemesia* 'Carnival' mixed.

138 *Phlox drummondii*, Annual phlox.

139 Border phlox 'Brigadier'.

140   *Phlox divaricata* 'Chattahoochee'.

141   *Potentilla* 'Wm. Rollinson'.

142   *Peltiphyllum peltatum.*

143   *Pyrethrum* 'Brenda'.

144   *Primula × juliana* 'Betty Green'.

145   *P. heladoxa.*

146   *P. polyneura.*

147   Polyanthus 'Pacific Dwarf Jewels'.

148 A *Lewisia howellii* hybrid.

149 *Primula japonica*.

150 *Polygonum amplexicaule* 'Atrosanguineum'.

151   *Rudbeckia* 'Marmalade' with dwarf China aster.

152 *Rudbeckia* 'Giant Hybrid Tetraploid'.

153   Rhodanthe.

154 *Salpiglossis sinuata* 'Bolero'.

155 *Saxifraga aizoon* 'Baldensis'.

156 *Viola* 'Jackanapes'.

157 *Stokesia laevis.*

158 *Tierella wherryi.*

159 *Stachys macrantha* 'Rosea'.

160 *Thymus serpyllum* 'Pink Chintz'.

161　Marigolds, French and
　　　African.

162　Marigold (African)
　　　'Golden Jubilee'.

163　*Tradescantia virginiana*.

164　*Zinnia elegans*, two modern
　　　types.

165　Pansy 'Floral Dance'.

166　Zinnias are featured in this annuals' border.

167 *Ursinia anethoides.*

DESCRIPTIONS

For a note on the way the descriptions are set out and Glossary of horticultural terms,
see *page 230.*
Numbers in **bold** *refer to colour plates. Dimensions in italic are in centimetres.*

Acanthus 8

These highly ornamental perennials, which have the unlikely common name of Bear's Breeches, during the summer months produce stately spires of tubular purple and white flowers from large-leaved clumps. Use these plants in isolation in places where a bold effect is needed. In addition these are fine background in a mixed border or even as we have used them as subjects that give height in a large rock-strewn bank. A well drained, moderately fertile soil is required. A little shade is tolerated and if your soil is dry or chalky these plants should grow well for you. Mulch the crown with leaves before the onset of cold weather in places where hard winters are likely. After several years growth the clumps may be divided up to obtain new stock, although propagation from seed is better. Gather the pods just before they explode sending the large seeds in every direc-

tion. After soaking in water overnight the seeds can be sown straight away using a cold frame for winter protection. We like to pot the seedlings when quite small and leave them undisturbed in these pots until large enough to plant out. By using this method the root disturbance is kept to a minimum.

—*mollis* is a fine species from Italy with large, glossy, non-spiny leaves and massive flower spikes. *110 × 90*

—*spinosus* has deeply-cut, spiny, rather hairy leaves. Spines are also present on the purple bracts which hold the generally white flowers. *120 × 110*

Achillea

These are perennials which grow well in ordinary garden soil including those that are alkaline. They prefer a well-drained sunny position. Such conditions are essential in the case of the flat-growing alpine sorts. Achillea's are sometimes also called 'Milfoils' (from *mille* a thousand) on account of their very finely divided ferny leaves. As an added bonus the leaves are frequently aromatic. Their stem height varies considerably according to species but their masses of tiny flowers are always arranged in a terminal corymb or head. Division of the often matted crowns when the plants are dormant is the easy way used to obtain fresh stock. The flower stems of *A. filipendulina* may be cut when the yellow is brightest and dried in the same way as is suggested for acrolinium (see p. 123).

— **'Coronation Gold'** is a fine border plant producing a succession of golden heads. *90 × 45*

— *filipendulina* **'Gold Plate'** produces tall, erect stems each with 15 cm wide plate-like heads of bright yellow florets. *110 × 60*

— **'King Edward'** has pale primrose flowers well displayed against the grey leaves. *15 × 25*

— *millefolium* **'Cerise Queen'** is a vigorous mat forming 'Yarrow' with large ovoid heads of deep cerise florets. *75 × 50*

— *ptarmica* **'The Pearl'** has stems of shiny green leaves bearing loose heads of white flowers.

60 × 75

— *tomentosa* is a fine species for the sunny rock garden. It bears a marked resemblance to *A. millefolium* but is more dwarf with softer leaves. The flower heads are deep yellow. Whilst with the dwarf plants it might be mentioned that there are some useful mat-forming plants with silver flowers to be found listed as *A. argentea*. *15 × 35*

Aconitum
The 'Monkshoods' are sturdy, upright, clump-forming border plants for sun or shade. They bear deeply cut, sometimes glossy green leaves and generous spikes of hooded, mostly blue flowers. All parts of these plants are highly poisonous to man and beast and for this reason should not be planted within reach of cattle. Although easily grown the monkshoods are better when planted in a soil that does not completely dry out and where it has been previously manured they will excel themselves. Each spring it is good practice to thin the shoots as they emerge selecting only the sturdiest for flowering, the clumps can also receive a good

mulch of compost at this time. Summer work consists of removing the flower spikes as these go over and finally cutting back all the stems during the fall. Poor flowers are usually due to overcrowding of the stems or too dry a site. New stock can be procured by dividing the black fleshy roots in the fall.

— 'Bressingham Spire' forms clumps of glossy leaves in the spring from which later the tall, narrow stems of rich violet flowers appear. *90 × 50*

— *napellus* 'Bicolor' has attractive pale blue and white 'helmeted' blooms. *100 × 50*

— — 'Carneum' is a less common sort of this variable species with light pink flowers. *100 × 50*

— *wilsonii* Originally from China and named after Dr E. H. Wilson who collected many fine plants there. These are tall, rather late flowering their tapering spikes of deep lavender blooms not appearing until the fall. *120 × 45*

Acrolinium

Correctly known as *Helipterum roseum* these are annuals with upright branches bearing whitish leaves and delicate pink or white daisy-like 'everlasting' flowers. Originally of Australian origin they are both attractive border plants as well as being much valued as a cut flower. Where these are required for winter decoration cut the stems before the flowers are completely open hanging the bunches upside down in an airy place to dry. Check on them now and then because they are sometimes attacked by mildew as they are drying. Damage is less likely where the bunches are gently eased apart at intervals during their drying. In warm soils the seeds may be sown during the spring directly where they are to flower. In colder parts the seeds must be sown in boxes; under cover for later planting out. A dry warm season suits these plants best for when it is cool and damp the leaves have a tendency to rot off rather easily. *45 × 15* **6**

Similar to the above but with larger flowers is *Helipterum manglesii*, or Rhodanthe. Obtainable in deep rose or white we prefer to raise these under glass growing the young plants on in pots before planting outside later. *45 × 15* **153**

Adonis

Not too often seen, these are plants with attractive leaves and showy flowers early in the season. Any light soil seems to suit them; they may be sited in the front of a mixed border, on the rock garden or even with shrubs. New plants come from divisions done in early spring.

—*amurensis* **'Plena'** is a Japanese plant with much divided ferny leaves in which the double yellow flowers will be seen nestling during early spring. *25 × 50*

——**'Fukujaki'** has shining orbs of clear yellow appearing very early in the season. *25 × 45*

—*vernalis* is a European native with large single yellow blooms. *25 × 30*

Aethionema 3

A dry well-drained sunny spot in the rock garden or niche in a stone wall suits these colourful shrublets best. Coming originally from Asia Minor they are not too tolerant of damp winter cold. For this reason it may be wise to take the precaution of protecting the plants with a pane of glass where this is practicable. If your soil is not naturally limy a little may be added to the planting area before setting out the plants. These have rather fleshy leaves. The masses of flowers which are produced over many weeks from spring to summer are carried in short, dense racemes. 'Candy Mustard', an old name for these plants, refers to the pink flower colour and the similarity of the individual tiny florets to that of mustard – a close relative. Cuttings of non-flowering shoots rooted in a pot of sandy compost and over-wintered under glass will make up into nice flowering clumps when planted out during the following spring. Our illustration taken in the Savill Garden, Windsor shows an association of the charming pink-flowered hybrid 'Warley Rose' which attains 15cm × 25cm, with thrift and *Saxifraga aizoon* growing together in a raised alpine bed.

Ageratum

The dwarf-growing cultivars of *A. houstonianum* the Mexican species usually seen in gardens are free and long flowering half-hardy annuals. Sometimes named 'Flossflowers', the individual flowers are like tiny powder puffs and are carried in really dense heads, at first on small compact plants but becoming rather more open as the season advances. They are splendid as edging plants in bedding schemes acting as a more muted foil for the strident reds of the salvia's and geraniums. To grow the best plants select a sunny, sheltered place with soil that does not dry out completely in hot weather. For a long season of flowering the seeds must be sown under glass then the seedlings pricked out in pots or boxes. Years ago cuttings had to be rooted during the summer and then overwintered in heat in order to keep the strain going for the next season. Fortunately this is something now no longer required for modern seed strains come 'true'.

——'Blue Angel' is soft blue perhaps with a suggestion of lavender. *12 × 25*

——'Blue Blazer' produces deep blue flowers on a compact, particularly even plant. *12 × 25*

——'Blue Mink' has mauve-blue flowers on taller plants.

20 × 35

——'Biscay' produces large heads of clear blue from an early age. *20 × 25* **15**

——'Fairy Pink' has rose blooms which is a break from the usual blue. *20 × 35*

——'Summer Snow' is a pure white version of 'Blue Blazer'. *12 × 25*

Ajuga

The perennial *Ajuga* species below are hardy, low, easily grown plants, thriving in moist soil whether it be sun or light shade. Although their chief merit lies in the coloured leaves produced in dense tufted crowns the flowers are pretty too. These are arranged in short upright spikes. Normally treated as rockery subjects they make good cover for odd corners. When using any of these low-growing plants for ground cover it is of course essential to ensure that every last piece of weed has been removed. To propagate, simply lift the plants and divide up the crowns as required.

—*metalica* or 'Crispa' has deep blue flowers and curled foliage with bright metal-like tints. This

125

is probably a form of *A. pyra-midalis*. *15 × 35*

—*reptans* is the 'Bugle' a familiar British wild flower of open,
moist woodland situations. Many
fine coloured leaf forms have been
introduced including 'Burgundy
Glow' – wine-red leaves;
'Atropurpurea' – rich purple;
'Multicolor' (or 'Rainbow') with
rose and cream variegation. *15×45*

Alchemilla 7
These are clump-forming
plants with decorative, soft,
rather hairy leaves and billowy
sprays of yellow or greenish
flowers. 'Lady's Mantle' will
grow well in normal soil in sun
or part shade, hot sunny places
are best avoided although we
have found them to be tolerant
of dry shade, an often difficult
place to furnish with plants.
Division of the clumps will
ensure new stock when needed, seeds may be sown where
plants are to remain – self-
sown seedlings frequently appear but not always where they
are wanted!

—*alpina* is a good rock plant
with silvery hairs cladding the
under surface of the lobed green
leaves. Greenish flowers in fairly
compact heads. *15 × 30*

—*mollis* with sulphur-yellow
flowers in large open sprays is an
easily grown border plant. *30 × 45*

— × *splendens* rather taller than
alpina which in some ways it
resembles, this hybrid is a dense
grower with silver veining on its
leaves. *25 × 35*

Althaea
A. rosea, known as Holly-
hocks, are those very tall,
familiar cottage garden flowers
that are so valued for adding
height at the back of a border
or for a quick summer screen.
Although really hardy perennials most gardeners prefer to
grow them as biennials discarding the clumps after
flowering during their second
season. An open, airy, sunny
site in deep rich soil means that
the plants can produce the best
stem height and consequent
floral display. Keeping to young
vigorous stock also tends
to lessen the risk of disease
which could be devastating.
Bear in mind that staking will
be required in exposed places.
These summer flowers are
available in many colours –
white, pink, purple and yellow
– both single blooms and
superb doubles. *240 × 60*

Alyssum

A group of yellow-flowered annuals and perennials of which only one, the familiar 'Gold Dust', *Alyssum saxatile* originally from eastern Europe, is normally met with in gardens. These are sub-shrubs delighting in a well-drained sunny situation. They are seldom better than when draping down over a dry wall. Their long grey felted leaves are a perfect foil for the light, almost fluffy heads of tiny golden flowers which reflect every ray of spring sunshine so well. These are not always long-lived plants; if straggling shoots can be shortened, after the spring flowers are over, and a more compact clump encouraged then the life of the specimen will be lengthened. New plants can be raised from seed which has to be sown very thinly in a light, airy frame. Self-sown seedlings frequently appeared in a gravel path which we formerly had. Named sorts can be raised by taking cuttings of shoots after flowering. Place these, say five to a pot, in gritty compost. After an initial watering they should have only sufficient to keep them from wilting until after the roots have formed. If the pots are placed in light shade the cuttings should root quite easily, and when planted out later the same season will soon make up into fine flowering plants.

—*saxatile* 'Citrinum' – also known as 'Silver Queen' for its light silver leaves and pale primrose-yellow flowers. *30 × 45*

——'Compactum' almost exactly matches the original species in colour, its bright golden-yellow flowers however spring from plants which naturally form compact mounds of grey leaves. *25 × 30*

——'Dudley Neville' with pale biscuit colour flowers is an unusual colour 'break'. *25 × 40*

——'Flore Plenum' has sprays of double golden flowers on a slow-growing plant. *25 × 30*

Alyssum maritimum of the seedsmen is botanically *Lobularia maritima*. These are the familiar, very free-flowering, honey-scented hardy annuals so useful for edging beds and borders. When sown or planted in well-drained paving or rockeries these will often self-sow themselves freely yet without becoming invasive. Seeds may be sown either where they are to flower, or in cold wet areas in boxes under glass for transplanting later. Well-drained, sunny positions will have the best plants for here a mass of tiny bloom will cover the stocky little bushes. Rich diet does not suit this group and leaves at the expense of flowers will result. A trim over with scissors when the first flush of bloom is past and before seed is set will spur on the plants to renew their flowering efforts. White alyssum is the usual plant seen. Rather less vigorous are the intriguing mauve shades which are worth experimenting with.

—— 'Little Dorrit' is upright rather than spreading with dense white flowers. *10 × 30*

—— 'Oriental Night' is possibly the finest of the purple sorts with even growth and an abundance of richly coloured flowers. *7 × 20*

—— 'Rosie O'Day' has a clear rose-pink head. *10 × 25*

—— 'Snowdrift' starts to flower early yet is a continuing mass of pure white. *7 × 20*

Amaranthus
A. caudatus ('Love-lies-bleeding or Velvet flower') is an easily-grown annual from the tropics with rich green leaves and long tassels of tiny, closely-packed red or green flowers. These are quick growers in good soil which is kept just moist, and they are most effective when used as 'dot' plants in a bedding scheme. We have sown these in the open and had plants for a late display but for general use would suggest that seed sown under glass is better. The young plants must not be planted until danger from frost is past. *90 × 45* **93**

Anagallis
A. linifolia is a very pretty half-hardy annual with intense blue or red flowers. Low bushy growth suggests using these as an edging, the rock garden is another place for a few of these as the blooms appear all summer long when many rock plants are over. Our rock garden which was sunny and dry supported a small colony of these delightful plants which kept going with self sown seedlings appearing with the

heathers for several seasons.
15 × 30

—*monelli* is a shrubby
'Pimpernel' from Spain with deep
blue flowers which is seen at its
best in a dry well-drained gritty
bed or scree. *30 × 40* **16**

Anchusa
The decorative, tall perennial
plants of this genus are derived
from *A. azurea.* They are
invaluable in the mixed border
not only for their height but
also for the wonderful display
of blue flowers they provide.
The tall flower stems emerge
from the tufts of long leaves
during early summer with the
wide, branching flower spikes
bearing blooms in all shades of
brilliant blue. These are sun
lovers thriving in well-drained
fertile soil. Some form of support will be essential, for left
untended the stems tend to
topple over. Cutting back
these stems as the flowers fade
frequently encourages a
second showing. They are
sometimes treated as biennials
and seedsmen offer packets of
seed for sowing one year for
the next year's flowers. Named
sorts are increased from root
cuttings (see page **41**). Heavy

soil combined with prolonged
wet winter weather is fatal for
these plants. If this combin-
ation is likely in your garden
we suggest lifting the roots and
overwintering them in sand
under a cold light. They are
quick growing and will make a
good showing when planted
up once more in the spring.

——'Loddon Royalist' produces dark blue flowers on sturdy
upright stems. *110 × 60*

——'Morning Glory' has deep
blue flowers each with a white
centre. *150 × 60*

——'Opal' is a pleasing shade of
pale blue. *120 × 60*

——'Royal Blue' bears brilliant
blue flowers. *120 × 60* **9**

Androsace
These are fine rock or wall
plants for cool climates which
form a mass of leaf rosettes and
bear dainty sprays of small
flowers. Cultivation requirements are a well-drained gritty
soil with added humus, a position in either sun or part-shade
and if at all possible some
protection from winter wet.
New plants come readily by
removing rosettes from established plants and rooting them

in gritty compost in a cold frame.

—*lanuginosa* is an easily-grown Himalayan species with spreading stems of silvery rosettes producing tiny sprays of pale pink flowers in late summer. *7 × 25*

—*sarmentosa* has larger rosettes than above and generous sprays of pink flowers each with a red eye. *10 × 20*

Anemone

The 'Windflowers' are a varied group of perennial plants which according to species are suited to cultivation in the rock garden, border or woodland. Providing it does not dry out ordinary soil suits them. All will benefit from the addition of leafmould or peat. New plants can be raised from seed sown as soon as ripe in pots under glass although it is not always the method in general use (see in individual notes below).

—*appenina* single and double forms either white or rose of this pretty spring-flowering plant can normally be purchased. Plant them in groups on the rock garden, shade suits them well. Increase: by dividing the tuberous rhizomes after flowering. *15 × 20*

—*blanda* has many-sepalled clear blue flowers in the wild plant with pink and red shades added to those in cultivation. Similar in appearance to the foregoing these winter and early spring flowers demand a warm well-drained loam in which to flourish. Increase: by division as above. *15 × 20*

—*coronaria* is the botanical name of which hybrids include the St Brigid and de Caen strains of the florists. Familiar colours are red, blue, lavender and white flowers each set in a green ruff. Although not particularly good for garden decoration (some may disagree) these are very good for cutting. Loamy soil and a partly shaded spot suits them best. Increase: by sowing the cotton-wool-like seed in moist soil. Small corms are readily obtainable and cheap to buy. *20 × 25* or larger.

— × hybrida (also known as *A. japonica*) are herbaceous subjects much valued for their late and long flowering from the end of the summer through fall. They produce stiff stems with deeply cut leaves; flowering is generous with the numerous saucer-shaped flowers composed of silky-backed sepals surrounding a central boss of golden stamens. 'Japanese anemones' succeed as well in sun as part shade when planted in light, fertile soil. The clumps spread steadily by means of their thick, woody roots but never become invasive. Plants should remain undisturbed, young transplants will most probably take a full season to establish and thus may not flower during their first year. Increase: by division of the roots or root-cuttings.

— — 'Honorine Joubert' has elegant single white flowers. *120 × 45*

— — 'Queen Charlotte' bears semi-double clear pink blooms. *80 × 45*

— — 'September Charm' is a particularly fine sort with single deep pink flowers each with a golden centre. *45 × 60*

— × *lesseri* is a garden hybrid which may be had in several colours, red or rose-red seems to be most popular. The comparatively large blooms are carried on upright stems on plants which thrive in a moist cool border. Increase: by division of the fibrous roots. *50 × 30*

— *nemorosa* is the 'Wood anemone', a pretty European (inc. Britain) native woodland plant which is always a welcome sight in spring. Variable in the wild although the nodding pink-flushed white flowers are the most com-

monly seen. Cultivated forms are in a variety of colours including a delightful pale blue. They may also be procured in different forms both single and semi-double. Plant these in the shade in soil that does not dry out at least until early summer. Increase is by division of the slender roots. *15 × 20*

Antennaria
The narrow silver-backed grey leaves are almost the main feature of *A. dioica* the species normally seen. These plants are hardy, forming dense carpets in poor well-drained soil. Use them on the sunny rock garden where they make fine ground cover for tiny spring bulbs. Increase is by dividing the crowns in spring.

— — 'Aprica' produces pure white fluffy flowers. *10 × 25*

— — 'Minima' is the tiniest of these small plants with its stems of pink flowers held hardly clear of the leaves. *8 × 20*

— — 'Rosea bears deep pink-puff like flowers. *10 × 25*

Anthemis
The kinds of 'Chamomile' described are a group of border or rock plants with divided

aromatic leaves and daisy-like flowers. They are easily grown in light well-drained soil preferably planted in full sun. Additional stock can normally be obtained from divisions of the old plants, sometimes cuttings of new spring shoots are used instead. Place these in sandy compost under a cold frame to root. *A. nobilis* and its non-flowering clone 'Treneague' can be increased in this manner and when planted out in sufficient quantity will form a springy, pleasantly scented lawn.

—*cupaniana* forms a wide clump of greyish leaves with comparatively long stems of large single white flowers. These plants for the large rock garden or border bear flowers intermittently over many weeks. *30 × 60* **2**

—*tinctoria* and ***A. sanctijohannis*** as parents have produced some splendid border plants with cut leaves and long stems of attractive single blooms. Plants are inclined to sprawl so remember to give them some support from early in the season.

——'Alba' bears creamy-white flowers. *75 × 50*

——'Grallagh Gold' is golden-yellow, fine for cutting. *75 × 50*

——'Kelway's Variety' produces rich yellow flowers. *75 × 50*

——'Mrs E. C. Buxton' has light lemon-yellow daisy-like flowers. *75 × 50*

Antirrhinum

The 'Snapdragons' are well-loved cottage garden flowers and in their present day forms are welcomed as first rate spring or summer bedding out plants. Although these are really perennials they are far better when treated as annuals. In Britain the usual system employed is to sow early in the new year planting the youngsters out in late spring. We prefer to grow these as biennials in which case starting off the seedlings the previous year is the rule. In countries where the winters are mild enough (and we are thinking of New Zealand in particular) the plants from these early sowings will commence their flowering season in mid-winter and continue on through until they are replaced with summer bedding late the following spring. When sowing there is no need to cover the seeds, simply sow on the surface of previously watered trays or flats. After the seed-lings have been transplanted pinch out the tops to ensure a nice bushy plant to set out. Their soil preference is for a well-drained fertile loam in a sunny place. There are many types and colours of snap-dragons available and a good seedsman's catalogue should be consulted to make your selection. Our two illustrations show different kinds, No **19** is 'Hummingbird' a delightful dwarf range and No **10** is the opposite end of the height range with flowers on stems some 75cm in length.

Aquilegia

'Columbines' are border and rock plants with graceful fern-like leaves and striking colour-ful flowers often sporting prominent 'spurs'. The border types are easy to grow in almost any soil although they tend to do better in moist rather than very dry sites. The smaller dwarf growers should be provided with a sandy loam to which some leafmould has been added. Cultivation of the tall plants includes mulching with old manure each spring and removing dead flowers as

these fade. These will grow in limy soils and shade is toler-ated very well. New plants can be grown by carefully dividing the forked roots. Young plants are easily raised by sowing seed in boxes and lining out the seedlings in the open ground as soon as large enough.

—*discolor* is a miniature alpine plant from Spain with dainty stems each carrying one or two blue and white flowers. *15 × 20*

—*flabellata* 'Nana Alba' has been developed from a Japanese species. It is suitable for the rock garden where the plants when in bloom are mounds of extra large snow white flowers. *30 × 20*

— × *hybrida* 'Crimson Star' has crimson, long-spurred flowers each with a white centre. *50 × 30*

——'Beidermeier' is an in-teresting strain with particularly heavy flower clusters. The indi-vidual blooms are in various bi-colours including red/white and blue/white. *40 × 25*

——'McKana Hybrids' is the ever popular seed raised strain with long-spurred flowers in a wide colour range. Red, blue, white, pink and yellow blooms can all be expected from a single packet of seed. *75 × 30*

133

Arabis

These are a large group within the family of crucifers. Although the common white-flowered sorts tend to be a little despised (perhaps because of the ease in which they grow?) few plants really provide such a mass of white in early spring as they do. In addition they grow virtually anywhere. Dry, well-drained sunny positions are ideal. Let them drape over a rough bank or decorate a rock bed; their evergreen foliage remains fresh if plants are trimmed back with the garden shears when the flowers fade. For a change they can be used as spring bedding plants under bulbs or as an edging to a planting of wallflowers. Propagation is from seeds sown in a cold frame during summer or by cuttings made of the non-flowering rosettes at almost any time of the year.

—*albida (caucasica)* is the frequently seen European species. The evergreen leaf-rosettes bear short stems of single white flowers in profusion over several weeks. The double form is a refined version. Named 'Flore Pleno', its flowers are larger although not as freely produced. *15 × 45*

——'Rosabella' A garden raised pink-flowered plant which associates well and is a useful contrast to the white sorts. *15 × 35*

Arctotis

These are annuals and half-hardy perennials originally from South Africa. When grown in dry, sunny borders they have showy flowers which are produced over a long season. Prolonged wet weather can cause rooting leaves in the perennials, the plants soon recover however when hot days return. The annuals are raised from seed sown either under glass for transplanting later or directly in the open in late spring. Thin these as they develop. Cuttings of the perennial kinds will root readily at any time of the year the plants are out of flower, late summer being preferred by ourselves. They should be dibbled in where the plants are to remain.

—'Hybrids' are fine perennials, most useful for covering dry, sunny banks. The large rayed flower-heads which close in the evenings are carried on stiff stems and are available in various colours from cream to deep red.

These are not winter hardy in Britain. In Australasia the flowers appear from mid-winter until mid-summer and intermittently at other times. *25 × 60*

— × *hybrida* the 'African Daisy' is a useful, long-flowering half-hardy annual. The daisy-like blooms appear in a wide colour range including white, buff, apricot and orange with blue discs. *30 × 25*

Arenaria
The *arenarias* are hardy, mat-forming rock plants for gritty, moist yet well-drained soil. Increase of stock is easy if small rooted patches are removed from established specimens and placed where they are to grow.

— *balearica* is an attractive carpeter with myriads of shiny green leaves. Although these are hardy plants winter frost sometimes kills them back a little however they soon recover. Plant these on the shady side of a large rock and you may expect to see the tiny white flowers appear over several weeks each summer. *5 × 20*

— *caespitosa* 'Aurea' (correctly *Minuartia verna var. caespitosa*) forms dense, very dwarf mats with

starry white flowers appearing above the greenish yellow leaves. Fine for rock or pebble gardens. *5 × 20*

— *montana* has prostrate stems of slightly hairy leaves with masses of comparatively large white flowers in early summer. Raise this one from seed. *10 × 25*

Armeria
A genus of low growing plants which form compact, tufted almost grass-like clumps. From the dense mass of leaves thin stems develop each spring to early summer each bearing a solitary flower head. These are frequently carried in such profusion as to almost completely obscure the foliage. These plants are almost indispensible in the dry, sunny spaces of the rock garden. Try them too as an edging for a flower bed. Propagation is effected by detaching shoots (divisions) after flowering and inserting these in very sandy compost ideally under a glazed light.

— *caespitosa* which is a native of Spain is a stunning little plant with the dense tufts of leaves sending up lilac flower clusters on short stems. Good drainage is partic-

ularly important for this one.
10 × 20 **12**

—maritima is the well loved 'thrift' or 'sea-pink' which is a variable plant native of the sea cliffs of Europe including Britain and for those of us old enough to remember was featured on the pre-decimal U.K. 3d. coin. *15 × 25* **3, 11**

Aruncus

These form imposing specimen or background plants with bold leaves composed of several leaflets and plumes of creamy-white flowers. They flourish in enriched soil in a moist, partially shaded border. Sited near water they are particularly attractive. An annual mulch of old manure spread around the roots each spring is most beneficial ensuring sturdy stems which can reach as high as 2m in the season. Cut these right down in the fall after flowering has ceased and the leaves are turning brown. If fresh plants are needed the clumps can be carefully divided at that time otherwise leave the plants undisturbed.

—sylvester (Goats Beard) forms large bushy clumps with white plumes. *150 × 50*

Aster 3, 4, 5, 14
(for the popular China asters see *Callistephus*)
The very large genus to which the perennial asters belong contains many valuable garden plants. Frequently they are called 'Michaelmas daisies' although in fact many flower before and after Michaelmas. Their height varies according to the species and cultivar and here will be found both the dwarf 'alpines' and tall border plants. Their flowers are showy varying in size from tiny star-like up to comparatively large – the size of a single chrysanthemum and each has a golden centre. The soil for the strong-growing border kinds should be well cultivated and manured for these vigorous plants quickly exhaust resources and require replanting every other season. After lifting the clumps retain only the best of the outer stolons for your new plants discarding any thin or worn out portions. An exception should be made with the *A. amellus* cultivars. These resent disturbance and can remain in position for four to five seasons at least.

Fortunately these root from

136

cuttings which can be made during the spring. The low growers require a free-draining soil in a sunny spot. Several of the tall growers will require staking. Although many of the garden forms have been raised and few plants are more typical of the English border almost all of the species from which they were derived are in fact native to North America.

—*acris* forms small bushes, the stems clad with narrow leaves and smothered in tiny blue-mauve flowers. *75 × 30*

—*alpinus* is a variable, always beautiful European alpine plant bearing large bright purple flowers on short stems. *15 × 20*

——'Beechwood' has blue flowers on a vigorous plant. *15 × 35*

—*amellus* are upright, bushy, summer flowering plants with rather rough stems and leaves and bearing large flowers each with a prominent central disc. Transplant these in spring.

——'King George' is a favourite of the group with large violet-blue flowers. *60 × 40*

——'Mrs Ralph Woods' produces splendid clear pink blooms.

60 × 45

——'Nocturne' has blooms in an unusual shade of rose-lavender. *75 × 45*

——'Sonia' also has large flowers this time they are clear pink. *60 × 40*

——'Violet Queen' is a compact grower with the golden centre of each bloom contrasting beautifully with the violet petals. *45 × 40*

—*cordifolius* are tall upright much branched plants bearing loose sprays of small flowers.

——'Silver Spray' is the plant of this section usually seen in gardens, its branchlets spangled with silver-white flowers. *120 × 50*

—*ericoides* form upright bushes of dark heath-like leaves with masses of tiny starry flowers in late summer and fall.

——'Ring Dove' has numerous mauve flowers. *80 × 50*

— × *frikartii* is a splendid hybrid with its light blue flowers each displaying an orange disc. *90 × 50*

—*linosyrus* (Goldilocks) is a British native with upright stems of dark green leaves and terminal heads of yellow flowers late in the season.

——'Gold Dust' is the refined version of the above which is a

137

useful contribution to the late border display. *60 × 45*

— *novae-angliae* have stiff, upright, leafy stems crowned with large single or semi-double flowers which are clustered in wide branching heads.

—— **'Elma Potschke'** which is a new introduction has large carmine-rose flowers. *110 × 45*

—— **'Harringtons Pink'** bears many soft pink flowers, flowers that remind us of childhood days and Church harvest festival services. *120 × 45*

—— **'Purple Cloud'** produces pale purple flowers each with a golden disc. *110 × 45*

— *novii-belgii* the true 'Michaelmas daisies' are upright plants with generally smooth leaves and stems which are branched only at their ends into heads of many flowers. These are at their best during fall until winter.

—— **'Ada Ballard'** bears large, double mauve-blue flowers. *90 × 50*

—— **'Blandie'** has semi-double white blooms. *120 × 60*

—— **'Carnival'** also has semi-double flowers, these are of a rich ruby-red shade. *60 × 40*

—— **'Chequers'** is violet – a splendid sort. *60 × 40*

—— **'Climax'** which is an old cultivar is so vigorous that it naturalises well even in rough grass. *150 × 50*

—— **'Freda Ballard'** has dark rather dusky red blooms. *90 × 50*

—— **'King's College'** is deep purple. *90 × 50*

—— **'Maria Ballard'** bears fully double light blue flowers. *90 × 50*

—— **'Mistress Quickly'** is a fine dark blue sort. *120 × 50*

—— **'Patricia Ballard'** has semi-double pink flowers. *90 × 50*

—— **'Prunella'** is reddish-purple. *90 × 50*

—— **'Royal Velvet'** is violet-blue, semi-double. *60 × 40*

—— **'Sonata'** produces very large light blue flowers. *110 × 50*

—— **'Winston S. Churchill'** is a particularly fine ruby-red kind. *90 × 50*

Dwarf *novii-belgii* are hybrids of particularly compact, neat growth. Use these very free-flowering plants in groups at the front of borders, as a dwarf hedge or on the rock garden where they make a fine show of colour from late summer until well into fall.

—— **'Audrey'** has large lilac-mauve flowers. *40 × 40*

——**'Blue Bouquet'** is bright blue. *30 × 30*

——**'Chatterbox'** bears masses of double, bright pink flowers. *40 × 40*

——**'Lady-in-Blue'** forms compact mounds of blue semi-double flowers. *25 × 30*

——**'Little Red Boy'** is very bright with its rose-red blooms. *35 × 40*

——**'Snowsprite'** is a good conrast with its semi-double white flowers. *30 × 40*

—*pappei* is a charming, much branched South African rock plant with bright green, rather thick leaves and masses of clear blue flowers for months. Not 100% hardy. *30 × 50*

—*thomsonii* **'Nana'** is a dwarf bushy plant with pale blue flowers each with an orange 'eye'. *45 × 50*

—*yunnanensis* **'Napsbury'** has rich blue, orange-centred flowers. Support for the weak stems will certainly be needed for this one. Good for cutting. *45 × 30*

Astilbe

These are a useful group of floriferous garden plants. Although individually tiny the flowers are borne in such num-

bers in the feathery upright spikes that their quantity more than makes up for the size. As the plants die down completely each fall we prefer to plant out and increase stocks during the spring, just as the deeply divided leaves are appearing again. It is a simple matter to split the clumps at this time, replanting the more vigorous portions in humus-rich soil. An annual mulch of peat or leafmould, together with a light dusting of an organic based fertiliser will be all that is required to keep the plants growing well for several seasons. Part shade suits them best for here there is less risk of the sun scorching the leaves as sometimes happens in exposed places.

Considerable variation exists between the several garden varieties both in their colouring and dimensions. Some of the diminutive forms which have solid poker-like flower spikes tend to creep over the soil. Site these in a moist shady spot in the lower part of the rock garden where their pretty unfurling leaves make a good foil for tiny early flowering bulbs. The taller growers, ideally planted in rich moist soil are fine for grouping in borders or placed by a pool or streamside where their plume-like flowers are reflected by the water. These also make good pot-plants particularly if they can be gently forced into flower for use indoors. Most of the garden kinds that we plant today are the result of crosses made between several Asiatic species by the French firm, Lemoine of Nancy, toward the end of the last century. Their pioneering work, which resulted in a wider range of colours than before, was continued a few years later by Georg Arends of Rondorf, Germany, His name is commemorated in the x *arendsii* which sometimes precedes the names of the popular cultivars briefly described below. The average size of these is *60 × 50*.

— — 'Cologne' produces bright carmine-pink spikes. 1

— — 'Deutschland' is a sturdy grower with pure white plumes.

— — 'Fanal' is compact, deep red spikes springing from clumps of dark leaves.

— — 'Federsee' bears bright rose-red flowers.

— — 'Fire' has glowing red blooms arranged in pyramidal trusses.

— — 'Irrlicht' with glossy dark green leaves sets off the ivory white of the flowers.

— — 'J. Ophorst' has tapering sprays with each ruby-red bloom displaying a purple glow.

— — 'Red Sentinel' with its stiffly erect red spikes spring from amid the dark purple leaves.

— — 'Rhineland' displays feathery plumes of clear pink.

— — 'Venus' has open sprays of pale pink.

— — 'White Gloria' is a free-flowering white variety.

— × *crispa* 'Perkeo' this choice plant has tiny spikes of pink flowers emerging from the mounded dark leaves each spring. *25 × 50*

—*chinensis* 'Pumila' grows easily in sun or shade if provided with the moisture at the roots that they need. These are spreaders sending up crowded lilac-rose spikes during the summer. *30 × 60*

—*glabberima saxosa* with its tiny, dense pokers of lilac flowers this is the ultimate in mini-sized astilbes and is quite in keeping with other plants in the smaller 'alpine' garden. Summer. *15 × 25*.

—*simplicifolia* 'Atro-rosea' displays shining pink flowers freely produced over the course of several weeks during the summer. *20 × 35*

——'Nana' is a delicate pink flowered miniature for a close-at-hand viewing position. *15 × 30*

——'Sprite' is less tall than 'Atro-rosea' above, this splendid hybrid raised in the Bressingham Gardens bears masses of shell-pink flowers above sheets of dark green leaves. *15 × 50*

—*taquetii* 'Superba' is taller growing than the x *arendsii* hybrids and these bear imposing plumes of rose-lilac flowers in summer. *120 × 60*

Aubrieta

The aubrietia's (note the slight difference between the spelling of the botanical name and that of the common name) or 'Rock cress' is a dwarf spreading, extremely showy, rock or border edging subject. From early until late spring each year the evergreen plants are completely smothered in flowers. Open sunny situations well away from overhead dripping branches suits them best. The named plants which we grow in gardens have been derived by the selection of distinctive seedlings of *A. deltoidea* which grows naturally in mountain regions from Sicily eastwards. We like to trim our plants back fairly hard as soon as the flowers fade. The clumps look bare at first but it is not too many weeks before they are completely green again. A mixture of fine peat and sand worked in amongst the shoots as they grow, after being cut back, will encourage these to make fresh roots. Some of these can be detached and potted up and if kept under glass for the winter will be ready for planting out in the spring. Where seed is being used for raising new plants this must be sown very thinly in a frame during the spring. We say thinly for these have a tendency for 'damping-off' disease to spread when crowded together especially under glass. Slugs and snails have also to be watched for as they are very partial to this group of plants.

——'Aurea Variegata' has each leaf neatly edged with cream and scattered blue flowers. *15 × 40*

——'Barkers Double' is pink

with a large proportion of semi-double blooms. *15 × 40*

—— **'Maurice Prichard'** is a delightful clear, light pink. *20 × 45*

—— **'Red Carpet'** is very foriferous and bears deep red flowers. *10 × 40* **13**

—— **'Triumphant'** is one of the best of the 'blue' shades. *15 × 40*

Bellis

The botanical Latin name for this, the 'Common Daisy', comes from *bellus* meaning pretty which must be a good name for these delightful little flowers even though they are lawn weeds in Britain! The variants of this hardy dwarf perennial have been grown in cottage gardens for many years, these making good plants for display from late winter until late spring. They thrive in normal soils and as well as for bedding they may be used for edgings, in window boxes or planters and in the rock garden. The seed-raised plants can be grown as biennials and discarded after flowering although, of course, these would last for several seasons but gradually diminishing in vitality. Seed should be sown in early summer for flowering the following spring. Named sorts are increased by detaching the crowns or leafy shoots after flowering and growing these on in a nursery row, transplanting them to their positions during the fall.

—*perennis* (seed-raised strains)

—— **'Fairy Carpet'** are in pink and white pastel shades. *15 × 30*

—— **'Pomponette'** have button-like blooms in mixed colours. *10 × 20*

In addition to these there are the 'Monstrosa' type which have large double flowers in white, pink and crimsom. *15 × 25*

(named cultivars)

—— **'Alice'** has baby-pink blooms with quilled petals. *7 × 15*

—— **'Dresden China'** is a dwarf with tiny pink buttons. *5 × 15*

—— **'Rob Roy'** could be termed a deep red counterpart of the above. *7 × 15*

Bergenia

Easily grown plants which each spring produce thick stems bearing open, bell-like flowers. The handsome, rounded evergreen leaves often turn from the usual lustrous green to deep red or vinous purple late in the season. Being long-lived plants they may be left undisturbed at the front of a border for many years. Good ground cover in virtually any soil is assured and as these thrive both in sun or part-shade much use is made of them for filling low maintenance beds in public parks etc. The old flowering stems can be removed after blooming is over and, apart from perhaps tidying the plants in spring by pulling off dead leaves, little needs to be done in the way of cultivation for the rest of the year. New plants are obtained by detaching well rooted crowns complete with a piece of stem. Take these just after flowering or later when the plants are dormant. When spacing out either for display or ground cover you should allow three clumps to each square metre. The leaves grow to approx. 30cm, the flowering stems slightly more.

—*cordifolia* was formerly known as *Saxifraga megasea*. The typical plants seen of the species has large heads of drooping, rather washed out pink flowers

— — 'Evening Glow' ('Abendglut') is very vigorous with glowing rose-red flowers.

——'Margery Fish' is a fine introduction named after a famous gardener. This plant bears large clear pink bells held on elegant spikes.

——'Morgenrote' has dense mounded growth with many short-stemmed salmon flowers appearing amid the round purple tinged leaves.

— — 'Purpurea' is a much better garden plant than the above with masses of light purple bells

— — 'Silberlicht' is a unique white flowered cultivar and like some of the other splendid named sorts is unfortunately rather hard to find in nurserymen's lists.

——'Sunningdale' bears clear red flowers on sturdy spikes. A plant with really bold leaves.

Begonia 18
For amount of flower and rich colouring there are few finer plants with which to grace our summer beds than the modern strains of tuberous – as well as fibrous-rooted begonias. Originally from the tropics, these are half-hardy perennials which require raising under

glass for planting out when the weather is warm. The soil should be rich, well supplied with humus and the plants will require water when the ground becomes dry. Most begonias thrive as well in part shade as full sun, how long they survive in the latter position depends on how well the soil was prepared for them. Seed sown in heat with a minimum temperature of 18°C early in the season will provide new stock. Very thin sowing is essential, simply sprinkle this into the surface of pre-moistened sandy compost. The plants have to be pricked out when tiny – a delicate operation – and finally planted out when the frosts are past. Sown early enough tuberous begonias will flower during their first season. Starting them off from purchased tubers is more usual. These can be placed on boxes under cover to allow them to sprout before planting out in the usual way. Fibrous-rooted kinds are also perennials, although these are being increasingly treated as half-hardy annuals to be discarded after their summer display is past. If a few roots are lifted at this time these make good house plants for flowering in the winter in a sunny window.

— *semperflorens* The modern F_1 hybrids are becoming increasingly popular for their even growth, long-flowering and weather resistance. They are compact and often with coloured fleshy leaves and masses of small saucer-shaped blooms.

— — 'Organdy' is a strain of mixed colours displayed against the green foliage. *15 × 20*

— — 'Galaxy' has bronze leaves with a mixture of red, pink, rose or white blooms. *15 × 20*
Individual colours (named clones) of both the above strains can be purchased.

— — 'Red Butterfly' is a new development in dwarf fibrous-rooted begonias with exceptionally large single red blooms. *20 × 25*

— — 'Red Diamond' produces its small red flowers freely all summer. *20 × 25*

— *tuberhybrida* (tuberous-rooted)

— — 'Fiesta' mixed (Multiflora Double) is a strain of relatively tough, compact plants which produces large, well-filled, fleshypetalled flowers in yellow, orange, pink and scarlet approximately six months after sowing. *25 × 20*

Brachycombe

B. iberidifolia, the 'Swan River daisy', is a half-hardy annual with much cut leaves and white, rose or blue flower heads. These are daisy-like, approximately 5cm across, each having a dark central disc. A native of Western Australia the Swan River daisy is a useful addition to the annual border or rock garden. They are easily grown in dry, sunny, well-drained places. Seed can be sown under glass for transplanting outside later or directly where the plants are to flower, thinning them out as required. *30 × 40* **17**

Calceolaria

C. **'Sunshine'** is a new development from the beautiful bedding calceolaria's which have yellow pouch-like flowers. They required overwintering under glass to be renewed from cuttings each season. With the introduction of this F_1 hybrid which even produces plants from seed the necessity for overwintering is eliminated. *30 × 30* **22**

Calendula

C. **officinalis** (pot marigold) is a hardy annual, seeds of which may be sown out-of-doors in virtually any sunny spot. In mild areas fall planting will provide an early display. The plants are compact at first and have large bright flowers now in unusual shades of apricot, rose and citron as well as the original orange. *40 × 50* **107**

Callistephus **21, 25, 26**

C. **chinensis** is the well-known, well-loved 'China aster', or simply 'aster' to many. These hardy annuals are valuable for summer to late fall, display in beds or borders, very good for cutting too. They come in a wide range of colours and forms these days ranging from the original large single daisy-like blooms each with its clear yellow disc to the 'mop-heads' of incurved chrysanthemum-like flowers. Others have innumerable tiny heads on bushy plants and some quilled or rolled petals. Colours vary from dark blue and purple to light pink, red and mauve, white and creamy-yellow. The soil for asters must be rich, loamy yet well-drained. Being shallow rooted they respond well to a summer mulch of well-rotted vegetable matter in the form of compost or old manure. Where disease is present it is inadvisable to grow asters on the same land for two seasons in a row. Seeds may be sown either under glass in spring (which is usual) or in the open ground in late spring as days warm up. Some representatives of the many different groups raised since the original introduction of this variable plant from China in 1731 are:

——'Giants of California' (Californian Giants) are late flowering with particularly large heads. *60 × 45*

——'Milady' is the name of a strain now available in three distinct colours: rose, blue and white. These form compact, bushy plants which are fine for bedding. *25 × 30*

——'Ostrich Plume' which is a strain having almost round flower heads with the central disc virtually absent or obscured within the long feather-like petals. *45 × 40*

——'Powder Puffs' have ball-like flowers in a wide colour range produced profusely on neat, up-right plants. *60 × 40*

——'Pinocchio' is a strain of extremely compact, floriferous plants bearing small bright flowers. *20 × 30*

——'Teisa Stars' have blooms composed of quilled petals in bright, clear colours. *25 × 30* **21**

Campanula 28, 29, 32

The campanulas, or 'Bell-flowers', are a very large group of border and rock plants. They bear various bell-shaped flowers (hence their common name) in shades of blue or purple and white. An exception being perhaps Canterbury bells some of which have clear pink blooms. The latter together with the cool greenhouse plant *C. pyramidalis* are biennials, the others described briefly below are perennials. They all share a liking for well-drained soil in either sun or part shade and a tolerance or in some a preference for those soils with an alkaline reaction. For the larger border plants, incorporate some old manure or compost in the soil when first planting out and mulch with a similar material annually. The tall sorts will need staking with pea-sticks in exposed places. Propagation of almost all kinds is by division. For some of the tiny growers small cuttings of young shoots are sometimes used. Slugs and snails are very partial to the emerging new growths and precautions have to be taken against these or plants will quickly disappear.

— *carpatica* 'Blue Moonlight' has prostrate heart-shaped leaves and upright stems of broad, bell-shaped blooms in a delightful shade of pale blue. *25 × 30*

—— 'Bressingham White' is a fine selection with pure white cups. *25 × 30*

—— 'Isabel' produces really deep blue-violet flat bells. Like other forms of *C. carpatica* these are suitable equally for the rock garden or border. *25 × 35*

— *cochlearifolia* is a justly popular rock plant with running stems and innumerable tiny light blue 'Harebells'. Easily grown in soil which is well supplied with humus. *C.c.* 'Alba' is a charming white version. *5 × 25*

— *garganica* has small open white-centred blue star-shaped bells both on the main clump and its laterally spreading branches. Plant these alpines in sunny rock crevices. *10 × 25*

— *glomerata* is a border plant with upright stems clad with rather large, hairy leaves and dense, rounded terminal heads of sessile (stemless) open-mouthed blue bells.

—— 'Superba' bears stems of clustered violet flowers. *75 × 35*

— *lactiflora* is a very tall species with upright stems bearing masses of small bells, a plant that is suited to edges of woodlands etc.

—— 'Alba' is a free-flowering white form. *150 × 60*

—— 'Loddon Anna' is a fine pink-flowered cultivar. *120 × 50*

—— 'Pouffé' is quite unlike the others in the fact that it forms a low mounded cushion studded with lavender-blue flowers. *25 × 30*

— *latifolia* is another tall growing border or woodland plant with bell-like white, purple or blue flowers according to the sort grown. *100 × 30*

— *medium* (Canterbury bells) are biennials which in their second season send up stout erect flowering stems bearing many long, rounded bell-shaped blooms in white and shades of pink, purple or blue. Plant these in fertile, enriched soil. 'Dead-heading' will prolong the flowering display. Sow the seed thinly in rows outside; thin out and transplant the young plants into nursery rows until finally planted out during the fall for flowering the following spring. *90 × 30*

—*persicifolia* is an evergreen species with tall stems of narrow leaves and large cup like flowers.

——**'Fleur de Neige'** has heavy double white bells. *90 × 45*

——**'Telham Beauty'** is clear blue. *120 × 45*

—*portenschlagiana (muralis)* is a very free-flowering, spreading plant for rock gardens or edgings. It bears tiny, toothed, smooth green leaves and masses of starry, upturned, light blue bells. *20 × 30*

—*pulla* forms itself into dense mats of smooth, round-toothed leaves from which spring countless stems of narrow, violet bells. *8 × 20*

—*turbinata* is often included with *C. carpatica* for they both carry almost flat bells. This one opens its large violet-blue flowers wide above the almost prostrate tufted leaves. *15 × 20*

Canna
These are colourful half-hardy plants which give a tropical air to summer display beds or borders. The fleshy rhizomes are planted initially during the spring in well-manured, moist soil. They are almost hardy so that in the milder parts of southern Britain may be left bedded outside permanently if so desired. It will be prudent to cover the crowns with litter for the winter months here. In New Zealand, where our illustration comes from, they are hardy over most of the two islands. But in places where cold winters are the rule they must be lifted after their summer display (just as soon as the first frosts have seared their leaves) and stored in moist sand in a frost-free shed. The plants may be started into growth once more during the following spring ready for re-planting outside later. Propagation of the named sorts is by division of the roots. The modern garden cannas are of hybrid origin. They bear striking colourful blooms in shades of pink, red, scarlet, orange and yellow often spotted with red. The leaf colour often enhances that of the flowers and instead of the usual green one may have rich maroon to rust brown-red. *90–150 × 60* **20**

Catananche
'Cupid's dart' so called on

148

account of an ancient use by amorous Greek women, is a short-lived perennial with flowers like cornflower. Blooms are useful both for cutting and also drying for winter use. Soil requirement is easy, provided that the site is well-drained and sunny. These plants may be placed in the border for a long succession of colour; we have seen them used as edging plants. New stock can be raised from root-cuttings although most find that seed raising will prove easier. Sow this early under glass and plants will be large enough to flower well during their first season of planting out.

—*caerulea* has flowers of purple-blue, white or lavender. *60 × 75* **33**

Celosia

Bearing dense, erect, plumed or crested flower heads these are very showy half-hardy summer bedding plants. They require a warm sheltered site with manured soil in which to luxuriate. Watering in dry weather will also be required if the plants are to grow well and to provide a continuing display of their unique flower heads. The taller kinds make interesting cut flowers and those bearing feathery plumes can be dried for winter arrangements. Seed must be sown under glass during the spring and after germination pricking out the young seedlings into sandy compost. Harden the plants well before planting out in warm weather during early summer. The kinds grown today are forms of *C. argentea* Plumosa, and *C. a.* Cristata.

——**'Coral Garden'** is an interesting mixture with long 'cockscombs' in a brilliant colour range. *40 × 30*

——**'Fairy Fountains'** are free-branching with plumes in shades of yellow, crimson, pink etc. *30 × 25* **23**

——**'Forest Fire'** is a suitable name for these bronze-leaved plants with striking orange-scarlet 'flames'. *45 × 30*

Centaurea

A very large genus with annuals, biennials and perennials represented. Although many of the almost 500 species recognised can be classed as weedy, others including the cornflowers and cultivated knapweeds are useful subjects both for garden decoration and cutting for indoors. The only soil requirements is that it should be well -drained. Tall kinds will need staking as insurance to stop them tumbling over just at the moment the flowers mature. These require division and replanting every three/four years. The annual cornflowers are hardy and can be sown out-of-doors, just where they are, to flower either during the fall or spring. Any fertile soil suits these as well. The taller sorts will need supporting with pea sticks.

— *cyanus* Although annual cornflowers now come in a wide range of colours it is probably true to say that original blue is still the universal favourite. **128**
There are two distinct height ranges:

——'**Tall Double Mixed**' is a strain providing flowers in blue, white, rose mauve up to 90cm.

——'**Polka Dot**' is a good mixture but at 40cm half the height of the above and less likely to blow over in exposed places.

——'**Jubilee Gem**' is an older well-loved favourite with bright

blue cornflowers on compact bushes. *30 × 40*

——'**Rose Gem**' is the clear rose version of the above. *30 × 40*

— *dealbata* '**John Coutts**' is a perennial with large clear pink cornflowers for many weeks during the summer months. *60 × 75*

——'**Steenbergii**' has striking rose-purple flowers. *75 × 50*

— *macrocephala* is a striking border plant with wide spreading leaves. The thick flower stems bear huge thistle-like yellow flowers which as well as providing an interesting display may be cut and dried for winter indoor decoration. *100–150 × 90*

— *montana* these are familiar border perennials with long silky leaves and upright stems of large cornflower-like blooms in various colours blue, white, rose etc., according to cultivar. *45 × 60*

Cheiranthus
These are a group of perennials many of which are treated as biennial. *C. cheiri*, 'Wallflower', is a long grown cottage garden favourite. Specimens may often be spotted with their roots firmly embedded in an old wall where they are truly perennial. As spring bedding plants they are best

when grown as biennials, sowing the seed outside during spring, thinning or transplanting later, then finally bedding out the now full-grown plants during the fall, ready for a fine display the following spring. A long growing season will develop husky plants, early transplanting ensures a good fibrous root system, pinching out the tops during their first year will make them branch into bushy specimens. When grown at home they can be transplanted with a trowel to keep the root-ball intact. These will grow away better than 'bunched' plants sometimes offered for sale. The botanical name is said to be derived from *cheir* (the hand) and *anthos* (flower) and originates from the early custom of carrying a nosegay of these scented blooms. They certainly have a delightful fragrance and in former times hundreds of acres of land in Britain were used for the production of cut blooms. In early books we read that 'the single wallflower is seldom met with only the double sorts being grown in gardens'. These had to be increased by taking as cuttings

the non-flowering shoots. For general purposes the opposite now applies for we raise single wallflowers from seed. Acid soils should receive a dressing of hydrated lime spread at the rate of approximately 6 tablespoons per 1 square metre. Perennial (named) cultivars are increased by inserting cuttings in gritty compost in either a sheltered spot out of doors or in a frame.

—cheiri (wallflower) is available in a wide range of colours including: red, yellow, orange, brown and purple. Some named cultivars come true from seed and there are both tall or compact sorts on offer from seedsmen.

——'Harpur Crewe' is a fine old yellow double flowered cultivar. Starting in late winter the short solid spikes of blooms are produced in succession for many weeks. *45 × 45*

——'Jacobs Jacket' is another good perennial. This compact, low mounded grower sends up flower spikes in a medley of colours including lilac, brown and orange. *15 × 45*

— × allonii 'Siberian wallflower' forms a dense clump of narrow green leaves and bears flowers of either orange or yellow in early summer. Although a perennial these are normally raised from seed each year as the plants frequently flower to such an extent that many of them do not survive as good quality specimens. 30 × 30

Chrysanthemum 31, 41

The genus *Chrysanthemum* is a large one containing annuals and perennials both herbaceous and shrubby. The hardy annuals, *C. carinatum*, *C. coronarium*, have daisy-like single flowers often marked and zoned in most attractive colourings. Their seeds may be sown in any light soil during the spring and it will be found that these develop into fine sturdy, well-branched bushes. If your plants appear to be growing tall instead of branching simply pinch out their growing tips. The perennials include *C. coccineum*, fine border plants generally known to gardeners as Pyrethrum. They are listed on page 210. *C. frutescens,* (Marguerite daisy) are shrubby plants with smooth almost evergreen leaves and virtually continuous flowering. The common white-flowered form is a useful summer bedder associating particularly well with scarlet geraniums and salvias. 40 × 45

C. maximum, (Shasta daisy) is another hardy plant for the herbaceous border and one valued for cutting. They all have white flowers, sometimes with yellow centres. Some favourite cultivars are: 'Esther Read' double, a popular commercial cut flower (75 × 50); 'H. Seibert' which has a large semi-double flower with twisting petals (75 × 50); and 'Wirral Supreme' which is also very large and fully double (90 × 50). The outdoor flowering 'Korean chrysanthemums' are, when compared to the Chinese forms, relative newcomers to Europe from America where they were bred. The early introductions were tall and very late flowering; the plants we grow today are dwarf and bushy-single and semi-double sorts are available. They form dense bushes almost as wide as they are high. Although these can survive outside during a mild winter the plants are better when lifted and kept in a frame for the cold weather. The cuttings made of the new shoots or divisions of the roots can be replanted in the spring. 70×60. The so-called 'Florist's chrysanthemum' has what is probably the longest recorded history of cultivation of any plant for according to the Royal Horticultural Society's *Dictionary of Gardening* we know that they date back to 500 B.C. in China and 800 B.C. in Japan. Although the precise ancestors cannot be traced with certainty, due to the great length of time since they were cultivated, there are still *Chrysanthemum* species growing in these countries. Like all of the other species in the genus these have single blooms. The modern autumn-flowering plants with incurved, reflexed, spidery and pompon forms have been evolved through the countless years by means of hybridisation, mutation and selection. The flower heads of the Compositae – daisy family – are composed of ray-florets, petal-like in appearance, (and usually incorrectly called petals especially by gardeners like ourselves!), and a pad of yellow disc-florets which forms the centre of the flower.

In the very modern double forms of chrysanthemum the coloured ray-florets predominate with very few disc-florets visible.

Some people leave their plants in place year after year. This is not the way to produce good plants with quality flowers. These have to be renewed from cuttings each season. Young plants which have been rooted from cuttings by the nurseryman are purchased initially. The spray types of early flowering chrysanthemums are suitable for decorating beds and borders. They normally arrive from the nursery in mid-spring. If they come by post it may well be that they are dry when they are received. If this is so, it is quite in order to place them overnight in jars containing a little lukewarm water. You will be surprised how well they will have picked up by the morning. The next step is to pot them up. We prefer to use a large peat pot, for these may be later planted out without a check to the plant. Use a well-drained mixture for potting and afterwards stand the pots in a closed cold frame. As soon as new roots appear at the sides of the peat pot will be the time to commence the hardening off process by leaving the light off during the day and finally off altogether. Late spring is the time to plant out into previously well-prepared soil. A sprinkling of hoof and horn meal, bone meal and sulphate of potash, in a mixture of equal parts can be sprinkled onto the soil surface and lightly hoed in. An additional small handful can be put under each planting hole as the plant goes in.

Many superior outdoor-flowering chrysanthemums have been introduced during recent years. Those which have large flowers after dis-budding are normally grown in rows where their staking and maintainance are more easily attended to. All our illustrations came from the Royal Horticultural Society's Wisley Garden, and what fine specimens they were! For general garden diplay the plants can be grouped in the border. Each must receive a cane (1m) and tied in carefully, early in the season. The small plants are stopped by pinching out the growing tip soon after they are planted, then once more during the summer (early to mid-June in Europe) this time pinching out the tips of all the lateral growths. After that they are left to grow on naturally making bushy plants with spray type blooms.

Chrysanthemums need firm planting in warm, moist, friable soil. They do not thrive in water-logged ground. If water is required during the growing season, give them a good soak and then allow them to almost dry out again before repeating. To combat insect pests spray the leaves and stems of growing plants regularly each week to ten days alternating the material between malathion and BHC (Lindane). As surface feeding roots develop as the season progresses one must be careful not to damage them when hoeing around the plants. In practice it is much better to mulch around the lower stems especially after mid-summer. Feed the plants at two week intervals with a proprietory chrysanthemum fertiliser, watering it in if the weather remains dry. Terminate all feeding when the buds appear. Later when the flowers are over will be the time to cut the stems down. Lift the stools and, after removing any remaining green shoots, plant the roots up into boxes. These remain in the greenhouse or frame for the winter months. Water them sparingly over this period. When the spring comes around the whole growing cycle is repeated by taking cuttings and rooting them in trays of sandy compost. **27, 35–40, 42–46**

Clarkia 79
C. Elegans and **C. Pulchella** are natives of North America where seedsmen have selected and bred many colourful forms of these popular (especially with children) easily-grown annuals. Colours include shades of pink, mauve, red and white in both single- and double-flowered blooms. Seed may be sown directly where plants are to flower, in any light soil, preferably in full sun. The young plants will require thinning or transplanting in order for them to bush out and form sturdy erect stems. Some light twigs may be needed for support. *60 × 45*

Cleome
C. spinosa (Spider flower) is a half-hardy annual, originally from the West Indies, which can form a large shapely bush when raised initially under glass and then planted out in rich soil in a dry, warm spot. The spidery flowers – white or pink in the cultivar 'Rose Queen' are fragrant and are carried for several months from mid-summer on. Use these plants on their own for a bold bedding display or to provide height in a mixed border of annuals. *60–120 × 45* **47**

Coreopsis
These are useful summer flowering annual and perennial border plants which, except for the named sorts, are easily raised from seed. Their flowers are showy, daisy-like on long stems, which makes most sorts good for cutting. A position in full sun placing them in light fertile soil will see the best plants develop. Seed of the annual sort should be sown in warmth in the spring if an early display outside is the aim, or they may be sown directly where they are to

flower rather later. Perennial kinds can be divided up when dormant; *C. grandiflora* tends to be short-lived if left to itself. We prefer to lift these each spring then replant only the best crowns. They can also be raised from summer-sown seed, transplanting the seedlings during the fall.

—*grandiflora* is the very large-flowered yellow perennial coreopsis (their common name is said to be 'tick-seed', but we only know them all as 'coreopsis'). Support their stems with pea-sticks and ensure that they have adequate water when it is dry. Some fine-named sorts have been introduced including:

——'Badengold' with strong wiry stems holding the rich yellow blooms. *45 × 45*

——'Goldfink' (Goldfinch) is a compact leafy dwarf grower with deep yellow blooms. *25 × 45*

——'Mayfield Giant' is deep golden-yellow. *45 × 45*

——'Perry's Variety' is a splendid semi-double clear yellow that we used to grow but have not seen lately. *30 × 45*

—*drummondii* Under this name are grouped some of the annual species often referred to as *Calliopsis*. These are easy to grow forming a delicate framework of branching stems covered with flowers in many different hues, yellows, browns, reds etc. *45 × 45* The dwarf forms of these make dense mounds with their tiny flowers also in bright shades including several 'tiger-coloured'. *15 × 20*

—*lanceolata* is a species from eastern United States which forms a well-branched bush (later) smothered in fine single yellow blooms. *75 × 60*

—*verticillata* is a perennial border plant with its branching stems bearing finely-divided leaves and masses of star-like yellow blooms. *45 × 45* **30**

——'Grandiflora' is similar but generally larger in all its parts. *60 × 45*

Cosmos 34
For fertile well-drained soil in full sun there are few less trouble-free annuals than 'Cosmea'. Recently manured sites must be avoided for here the danger is that all you will get are mounds of fine filigree foliage with sparse flowering. The annuals that we grow today have been derived mostly from the Mexican *C. bipinnatus*. These can be raised

156

under glass but like us most people find them easy enough when sown where they are to flower but of course thinning them well to ensure sturdy stems.

——'Diablo' is a kind that we have recently tried with semi-double fiery-red petals surrounding the bright golden centres. *60 × 45*

——'Sensation' is a strain with mixed single flowers in rose and purple shades and white. These are good cut-flowers. *90 × 60*

Dahlia

The garden dahlias are one of the more important groups of summer and autumn flowering plants. The species originally sent from Mexico to the Botanic Garden, Madrid in 1789, together with later introductions after considerable work by hybridists in Europe and America, have given rise to the diverse and colourful plants we grow today. Dahlias are half-hardy herbaceous perennials with erect branches, bold glossy foliage and strong flower stems. Their annual growth and consequently height varies according to the kind grown.

There are basically two groups: bedding dahlias, and the so-called tuberous dahlias. The latter are extremely variable and are divided into sub groups of many beautiful and diverse forms. Bedding dahlias originally with single, bright flowers were introduced to gardeners in about 1922. These can be raised from seed sown under glass during early spring, planted out when danger from frost is over, and after enjoying their bright display of flowers they are finally discarded in late fall. Use exclusively in beds of their own or in groups of perhaps 5 or 7 in company with other summer flowers. Due to their origins all dahlias can be regarded as sub-tropical plants which revel in bright sunshine with shelter from cold winds. Naturally any hint of frost will blacken all aerial growth. They delight in rich well-manured soil together with ample supplies of water during hot weather. Preparation of the site – especially for the large group of named dahlias – can begin several months before planting by digging in plenty of well-rotted manure or compost. Do not delay this type of preparation until planting time as rank, lush growth with few flowers could result. Dahlias respond well to summer mulching and at that time it will be in order to use manure or straw etc. on the surface for this. These taller dahlias being cultivars do not come true from seed so the tuberous roots must therefore be kept from year to year in order to maintain the stock. Cut the stems down after hard frosts blacken them during the fall, heaping them over the crowns for one or two weeks in order to ensure that the roots are well-ripened and able to grow away strongly the following spring. Later lift the roots, label them and dry them off under cover. Remove all the dry soil before storing them in dry leaves, peat or straw. When the spring comes around they are removed to a light place in the warm greenhouse and the lower part of the tubers plunged into moist peaty compost. We always dust the crowns with a fungicide at this stage to keep a check on disease. Keep the atmosphere moist by syringing staging, boxes and tubers; within a short while new green shoots will appear. Cuttings of these root readily at this time of the year. They should be taken with a small 'heel' of the old crown. The tubers may also be divided if only a few plants are needed. To do this wait until the new season's buds at the base of the old stems have swollen, then separate them with a sharp knife. It is as well to bear in mind that the tubers themselves are simply storage roots and as such do not produce new buds (which appear only from the woody portion of the old stem). These divisions may be planted out without further growing. When the time comes for planting, put your strong stake in first and when the young plant has grown large enough tie loosely to it. This will also be the time to pinch out the leading tip to make the plant 'break' into 3 or 4 stems. These can also be tied in as they grow by looping each to the stake individually. Use the tuberous dahlias in large beds on their own, with shrubs or in herbaceous borders where they make a fine show in late summer. Spacing depends on height. Allow approximately half of their ultimate height between the plants. Some of the flower types, in a wide range of colours, are as follows. Single, which have a single row of 'petals' (correctly known as ray-florets) surrounding the central disc of stamens (or disc-florets). Anemone-flowered, have flat outer petals around the mass of shorter, tubular florets. Peony-flowered have two or three rings of petals around their central disc. Ball dahlias are fully double flowerheads composed of tubular, blunt-mouthed 'petals' (or disc-florets). Pompon are similar in shape to the ball type but with more and smaller flowers. In the Collarette forms there are additional florets in the form of a collar usually in a contrasting colour between the outer 'petals' and the central disc. Cactus dahlias have double flowers with the often narrow, pointed 'petals' quilled for more than half of their length. In the semi-cactus section the generally broader petals are quilled for less than half their length. Of the several decor-ative types the formal decorative is double with the often rounded, broad petals arranged in a neat regular pattern. Informal decorative present flower heads of a tousled appearance with their arrangement of flat or slightly twisting, pointed 'petals' arranged in an irregular way. The above is only a very brief and incomplete summary of these colourful plants. For additional information consult the catalogue of a specialist nursery. The colour plates are photographs of dahlias taken in the Royal Horticultural Society's gardens, at Wisley, Surrey, England. **48–56**

Delphinium 57–64

Including 'Larkspur' these are familiar and well-loved summer flowering annual and perennial border plants. Their upright stems bear deeply cleft, somewhat hairy leaves and spikes of spurred flowers. In the elatum group the blooms are carried in closely-packed spikes whereas those of the belladonna type are presented in open spikes and can be of a more dainty appearance. Delphiniums thrive in soil well-prepared with old manure or compost. They prefer a sunny, protected place, well-drained yet remaining moist during a dry spell. Staking is essential for all delphiniums. The elatum group will need a strong cane to each stem; for specimen flower spikes it is usual to reduce the number of shoots appearing in the spring. How many to leave depends on the cultivar and age of the plant. Pea sticks will normally suffice for supporting other groups. New plants of named cultivars can be raised by rooting cuttings of the new shoots when they appear in spring or dividing up the woody rootstock when the plants are dormant. Named kinds of the Pacific hybrids will come true from seed. If a good strain is selected seedlings from the other groups will present a delightful range of colours and heights. Take precautions against slugs for they love the emerging shoots. Mildew can be a problem in some seasons. To combat this, spray with a recommended fungicide at two week intervals. 'Annual Larkspur' which have been

derived from *D. ajacis* and *D. consolida* are vigorous hardy annuals thriving in almost any well-drained soil. There are two distinct height ranges. The tall sorts (plate **56**) are useful for cutting. *75 × 35.* 'Dwarf Rocket' (Plate **57**) is a strain of neat-growing plants with blooms in shades of red, pink, white lavender and blue. *30 × 25.* Few plants respond as well as larkspur to the removal of spent flower spikes which prolongs the flowering season of the plants considerably. Sow the seeds in late summer in order to grow the best compact shapely plants. They prefer a sunny spot in which to display their flowers the following summer.

elatum group

— **'Blue Tit'** has dark blue flowers each with a white eye. *120 × 60*

— **'Butterball'** creamy yellow with a pale eye. *160 × 60* **61**

— **'Shimmer'** has a white eye in the centre of each light blue floret. *140 × 60*

— **'Vespers'** also with a white eye but with blue and mauve overlapping petals. *140 × 60*

belladonna group

Pacific hybrids

— **'Black Knight'** is the deepest blue with white eye. *120 × 45*

— **'Blue Bees'** is light blue. *110 × 45*

— **'Blue Jay'** is mid-blue with white eye. *120 × 45*

— **'Bonita'** has clear blue flowers. *110 × 45*

— **'Galahad'** is white. *120 × 45*

— **'Pink Sensation'** has clear rose pink flowers. *110 × 45*

Dianthus 67, 69–72

The Latin name covers pinks, carnations and sweet williams etc. These are all familiar garden plants beloved for their generally neat growth, delightful colours and scent. Few rock garden plantings would be complete without a selection of the dwarf alpine species. Others can be used for bedding and edgings and the taller growers are good cut flowers. Light well-drained soil in sun or part shade suits most *Dianthus*. In our former garden we grew particularly fine pinks in the lime-rich soil produced by the addition of mortar rubble and ashes over the centuries. The many species can normally be increased by sowing seeds either in the open or under a glass frame. Most of these will also grow from cuttings of tip or side shoots – a method which is essential for the named cultivars.

— **alpinus** forms grass-like green mats with short stems bearing single pink flowers each with a purplish zone of spots surrounding the eye. *15 × 20*

— **barbatus** (sweet william) are colourful biennials with masses of scented flowers. Use these in beds either on their own or with other plants. Seedsmen list several distinct strains of these excellent cut flowers. *35 × 40*

— **deltoides** (maiden pink). These are rock plants forming a green, grassy carpet. Slender stems bear small single flowers in several bright shades of pink, red, purple and, rarely, white according to the named cultivar selected. *25 × 30*

— **neglectus** is a European alpine, bearing cherry-rose blooms above the dense mat of leaves. *20 × 15*

Pinks, carnations etc. As is the case with several other flowers with a long history of cultivation which we grow today, are the result of a considerable amount of hybridisation over very many years. For convenience they are divided into different groups although overlapping is bound to occur here and there. First, carnation derived initially from *D. caryophyllus* these comprise: the perpetual flowering or florists carnations as well as border carnations which we grow in our gardens. The latter are hardy plants with strong silver-grey narrow leaves and scented flowers of classic shape in a variety of colours according to the named cultivar. Unlike some of the other carnations these flower but once a year – early summer. The Annual or French carnations are generally less hardy with masses of colourful, often scented blooms in succession and although similar in appearance to Border carnations these have inferior individual blooms. Next comes the Allwoodii or Modern pink. These are a splendid race of continuous flowering pinks raised originally by crossing the old white Fringed pink (*D. plumarius*) with the Perpetual-flowering carnation. These come in a wide colour range and many named clones are available. They can normally be identified by their 'Christian' names such as: 'Doris', 'Derek', 'Joan' etc. All are excellent plants for edging borders as well as for cutting. *30 × 35*

A further division within this group are Allwoodii Alpinus. Usually termed Rock pinks they are the result of crossing *D. x allwoodii* with various dwarf alpine species and what super little plants they are! Compact, colourful and free-flowering. Several choice sorts have been named. *15 × 25*.

Our next group comprises the Old-fashioned pinks. Not as popular as formerly due no doubt to the fact that unlike the Modern pinks they generally flower only once a year. They have great charm however and space should be found for them in the border or rock garden. Try, 'Musgrave', a single white with green eye; or 'Dad's Favorite' which is a semi-double white with red lacing and chocolate zoning. *30 × 35*. Lastly in this brief

162

survey are Hybrid dianthus. These have a very involved parentage including sweet williams and × *allwoodii*. They are often raised from seed and sometimes sold simply as a mixture although several named kinds belong here. They are generally colourful and easy plants to grow.

Digitalis 59
The foxglove as well as being a favourite cottage garden flower is a familiar woodland plant in many parts of Britain, where imposing stems made up of masses of purple tubular bells are a colourful sight in early summer. Although classed as perennial most of the species grown tend to be rather short lived. For this reason it is suggested that in the case of *D. purpurea* especially they are treated as biennials sowing the seed early in the first season, pricking out and finally transplanting into leafy soil in sun or part-shade when ready. Unless seed is particularly required, cut down their flower spikes as they fade and you may be favoured with an additional flush of bloom later in the season.

—*ambigua* is a pale yellow-flowered foxglove, the blooms curiously netted in brown. *60 × 50*

— × *mertonensis* has strawberry-pink flowers and makes a good border plant. *90 × 30*

—*purpurea* 'Excelsior' is a strain which bears long tapering spikes of spotted creamy-white pink or purple blooms. *150 × 40*

Dimorphotheca
These are half-hardy annuals and sub-shrubs originally natives of southern Africa which as may be expected thrive in warm, well-drained gardens. The colourful annuals, listed in seed catalogues as *D. aurantiaca*, are in fact derived from perhaps two additional species. They can be sown where they are to flower, thinning out as required. The colour of the calendula-like blooms is basically orange, although cream shades and purple zoning is often seen in their colouring. *35 × 45* **65, 66**

—'African Beauty' which is nearly hardy, is a low evergreen sub-shrub which will be found very useful for clothing dry banks or for planting on the larger rock garden. The comparatively large flowers have pinkish-white petals, with purple reverse, surrounding a metallic blue disc with orange stamens. Cuttings of this plant root with comparative ease at any time of the year. *30 × 45* **68**

Doronicum

Each year 'Leopard's bane' is one of the first border plants to flower in the spring. The stems of clear yellow flowers appear from tufts of tiny green leaves which become larger as the season progresses. Doronicums are easy-to-please perennials thriving in most situations. At one time we had them naturalised in light woodland where they competed for space with bluebells, wild *Narcissi* and Solomon's seal. The soil should be enriched with well rotted manure for better quality flowers; annual mulching will improve these too. Slugs and snails are particularly partial to the woody rootstocks and new shoots. Dividing these roots in spring will produce new plants as required.

— *cordatum* is a montane species from south-east Europe and Asia Minor with nearly heart-shaped leaves and wide golden 'daisies' on short stems. *20 × 30*

— — **'Harpur Crewe'** is a free-flowering plant with its yellow flowers well-displayed on stout stems. *90 × 40*

— — **'Miss Mason'** has light yellow blooms and is lower in height than the above. *45 × 45*

— — **'Spring Beauty'** with large fully double golden flowers. This is the outstanding doronicum, one whose reappearance is eagerly awaited each spring. *45 × 45*

Dracocephalum 116

D. ruyschianum The species described is upright, bushy, bearing narrow leaves with purplish-blue whorled flowers, arranged in long spikes. These are hardy border plants of similar appearance to, but rather larger than, nepeta the familiar 'catmint'. Well-drained soil in sun or light shade suits these easy growing plants which are so valuable for colour contrast in the border. Increase is by dividing the roots when dormant. *40 × 30*

Echinacea

These are sometimes seen listed as *Rudbeckia* which are close relations. They are hardy border plants and, like *Rudbeckia*, the flowers are composed of drooping petals arranged around the central cone. In the cultivated forms of *Echinacea* these blooms are larger and in a completely different colour range to most *Rudbeckia*. Plant these in light fertile soil in the full sun either in groups or singly. An annual mulch will be appreciated. As their stems are usually stout, staking will only be required if the site is particularly windy. Propagation of the named sort is by division of their roots when dormant. Seed can also be tried.

— *purpurea* 'Bressingham Hybrids' is a superb strain with the many warm rose-red flowers and orange central cone. *90 × 50*

—— 'The King' is an older favourite with the stout stems bearing black-centred magenta flowers. *110 × 50* **75**

—— 'White Lustre' is a rare and unique white form. *80 × 50*

Echinops
The perennial 'Globe thistles' with their large greyish leaves and tall stems of metallic-blue flowers are useful border plants. When the flowers appear it is not difficult to see how their botanical name was decided as they are round and quite spiny and *echinos* hedgehog, and *ops* – similar to, is most appropriate. These flower stems may be cut and dried as 'everlastings'. Globe thistles are long-lived plants thriving in almost any soil including alkaline. They grow best of all when sited in well-drained fertile loam enriched with decayed vegetable material. A sunny position is also preferred. To increase your stock divide the deep thistle-like roots when the plants are dormant.

— *humilis* **'Taplow Blue'** forms bushes of cobwebby grey leaves bearing stems of large round blue flowers. *150 × 60*

— *ritro* is the usually seen blue-flowered Globe thistle. Plant these either singly or in groups. *110 × 60* **78**

— *sphaerocephalus* requires plenty of room to develop its wide branching system of stout stems, shiny green leaves with felted reverse and large round grey flower heads. *210 × 90*

Echium
Our illustration shows a small

group of the annual *E. planta-gineum* 'Blue Bedder'. This makes a fine splash of brilliant blue continuing for many weeks of the summer from a spring sowing. These are hardy annuals and seeds may be sown broadcast where the plants are to flower, thinning them out as the leaves touch. A light free-draining sunny spot is best for them. Here they make up into nice little bushes. *30 × 30.* **66**

Erigeron

A large group of easily grown border and rock plants with flowers similar in appearance to the Michaelmas daisies but rather earlier flowering. All seem to do better in sunny places although here they require moisture retaining material in the soil and water during a dry spell. Most are hardy, perhaps the exception being *E. mucronatus*, for this, although it runs about happily enough in our Auckland, N.Z. garden was usually killed back in England. The border sorts make splendid cut flowers.

—*alpinus* is a low, spreading rockery or front of border plant with wide blooms composed of numerous purple petals surrounding the golden disc florets. *15 × 40*

—*macranthus* is leafy, upright and has blue-purple petals arranged around the yellow centre. *50 × 30* **74**

—*mucronatus* is a pretty almost ever-flowering Mexican plant which spreads itself around by means of underground runners. Give this a cool root-run and you will be rewarded with masses of white daisies with purple reverse to the petals showing as they close for the night. *15 × 30*

—*speciosus* hybrids. These are available in a wide range of colours and heights. All are particularly good border plants sometimes remaining in flower for two or more months. *45—60 × 40*

——'Charity' is a fine plant in the 'ity' Series (see 'Dimity' etc. below) all raised at Bressingham by Alan Bloom. It bears its light pink flowers erect on tall stems.

——'Darkest of All' true to its name has deep violet-blue flowers.

——'Dimity' bears large pink blooms on a small bush.

——'Foersters Leibling' is a rich pink, semi-double.

——'Prosperity' is a pale blue and also semi-double.

—— **'Quakeress'** has silvery-lilac flowers.

—— **'White Quakeress'** bears its white flowers over many weeks.

Eryngium

Striking plants with cylindrical heads of flowers each sporting a spiny ruff. These generally have a metallic blue or silver sheen with the colour extending down their stems. Deeply serrated leaves are an added feature. The flowers dry well for winter use. Well-drained sandy soil suits these border plants best. Increase is by dividing the clumps in early spring, root cuttings and seeds.

—**alpinum** is a European plant of deeply cut leaves, green below with the upper part of the plant and flower soft blue. *75 × 45* **76**

—**bourgati** is a beautiful blue hardy plant found wild in the Pyrenees. *45 × 30*

—**giganteum** bears silver grey leaves with many branched stems of spiny blue flowers. *110—130 × 60*

—**tripartitum** has grey-blue cone-shaped flowers carried amidst a spiny circlet of leaves. *90 × 60*

—**variifolium** produces branched stems of silver-blue flowers from its clump of marbled evergreen leaves. *75 × 35*

Eschscholzia

E. californica, 'Californian poppy) is a most colourful, easily-raised annual which thrives in beds, borders and rockeries. The sight of the wild plants with their myriads of open, funnel-shaped rich yellow blooms is said to have suggested the name 'The Golden West' to early pioneers trekking across the U.S.A. Today, as well as the golden shades, there are pinks, white and mauve in both single and semi-double forms. These are hardy plants which may be sown in a sunny well-drained place the previous autumn ready for an early display. They tolerate really dry places, the secret being to sow early and thin two or three times as the leaves just touch. Many fine strains are available including 'Art Shades' a group of which are featured in plate **73**. *20—30 × 15.*

Filipendula

These plants were long included with *Spiraea* and also have similarities to *Astilbe*. The small genus *Filipendula* contains variable plants all with attractive foliage the leafy stems bearing panicles of tiny flowers. Their preference is for either a damp site or soil that is well laced with rotted vegetable matter. Part-shade is tolerated well and will result in longer lasting flowers. The normal method of increasing plants is by division of their roots when dormant.

—*hexapetala* (Dropwort) has attractive ferny foliage and loose heads of creamy-white flowers often tinged red on the reverse of the petals. This plant will grow equally as well in dry, chalky soil as in moist. 'Flore Pleno' is a fine double flowered form perhaps seen as much as the single sort. *80 × 45*

—*purpurea* is a tall plant with large leaves composed of several leaflets and upright stems of rose-pink flowers during the summer. *110 × 60* **80**

—*ulmaria* (Meadow Sweet) a British native plant which is useful for damp areas in the wild garden. The flowers are white carried in a compound head. 'Aurea' is a golden foliage version

with possibilities as a contrast plant for other moisture-loving species. *45 × 30*

Gaillardia 114

A most useful genus of annual or perennial border, bedding and cutting flowers. All have very showy, daisy-like blooms freely produced in various shades of yellow, orange, and fiery-red. Position the plants in the sun and for preference plant them in light well-drained soil. Annual sorts may be sown out-of-doors in warm areas, otherwise raise them under glass for planting outside later. Perennials can also be grown from seed although in this case the named cultivars do not breed true. These will be found to come away readily from divisions of their crowns during the spring. The tall perennial kinds will need light staking to keep the blooms clean and mud-free. Annual strains developed from hybrids of *G. aristata* and *G. puchella* includes:

—**'Blood Red Giants'**, red. *45 × 30*

—**'Lollipop'** bears double flowers in mixed colours. *45 × 30*

Perennials developed mainly from *G. aristata* include:

— — **'Dazzler'** orange-yellow with maroon centres. *60 × 40*

— — **'Goblin'** is a mini-size with each yellow petal tipped in red. *15 × 25*

— — **'Mandarin'** has yellow petals heavily overlaid in flamered. *90 × 50*

— — **'Wirral Flame'** has red petals with pale yellow tips. *60 × 40*

Galega 114

'Goats Rue' are upright, rather bushy plants, their leaves composed of many small leaflets. Erect stems bear spikes of pealike flowers. Originally introduced into gardens from southern Europe and Asia Minor in 1568 *G. officinalis* has produced some fine variants which all make splendid garden plants. They are easily grown in almost any soil although better specimens will be seen where proper cultivation has been done. A mulch in early spring will result in longer stems, better foliage and masses of flowers. Some light staking is suggested for these for although their stems are usually quite sturdy they can become top-heavy with the amount of flowers produced. Plants are best left undisturbed for several seasons until the clumps appear to have become too thick and crowded. Splitting the roots when the plants are dormant will furnish new stock. Seeds may also be sown outside during the spring.

— *officinalis* **'Hartlandii'** has flowers larger than most in racemes some 10cm to 15cm in length. The pea-shaped flowers are lilac-blue and white. *90 × 60*

Gazania

For sheer amount of large colourful flowers during the late spring and summer there are few plants to equal the display put on by the progeny of *G. × splendens*, 'Treasure flower' or 'Black-eyed Susan'. Originally from South Africa these are low growers, their leaves green with silver reverse or occasionally completely silver. Their 13cm wide flowers are daisy-like in form and range in colour from cream to pink, orange, mauve and yellow – there is a particularly attractive double form of the latter. Our favourite must be *G.* 'Tresco' which forms compact silver-leaved clumps bearing large single apricot-yellow blooms.

G. × *splendens* itself has rich orange flowers each with a dark central zone. The best displays of these plants appears to be in sea-coast localities where they are growing in full sun on often dry sandy or poor clay banks. They do not tolerate rich soils for too long nor can they stand poorly drained soils at any time. Gazanias can only remain as permanent planting in favoured places and where much frost is likely they have to be overwintered under glass. Young selected plants are best for this. They are produced by taking 'Irishman's cuttings' (crowns complete with a few roots), dibbled-in with a little sand when the flowering season is past. Plants may also be raised from seed sown under glass during early spring.

Gentiana

The 'Gentians' form a very large group of plants including some of the choicest inhabitants of the rock garden that we have. Not all are the easisest of subjects to grow but those gardeners who can provide the correct conditions never fail to be rewarded by the superb display of glorious blue trumpets that are the feature of those described below. Lime-free soil is essential. One that remains moist yet is well-drained and has peat, leaf-mould and grit mixed into it before planting is also important. Sunny or partly-shaded rock gardens, peat bed or trough garden are some of the places where gentians flourish. Dividing the roots or very fresh seeds are two ways of increasing your plants. Seed should be sown thinly in pots, the compost comprising equal parts of fine loam, leafmould and sharp sand. Stand the pots in a shaded frame and pot up the seedlings as they appear. If few or none germinate allow the pots to be exposed to frost and snow the following winter before replacing the frame covers once again.

—*acaulis* this is the 'Trumpet gentian', a native of European mountains. The large, stemless, funnel-shaped blooms are an arresting sight as they appear in the early spring. *7 × 30*

—*septemfida* More erect than the foregoing, this summer flowering species bears several stems of clustered blue flowers. *30 × 30* **81**

—*sino-ornata* are prostrate growers with their stems ascending only at the ends. The comparatively large open-mouthed, funnel-shaped flowers are clear deep blue with dark blue bands running down the length of the corolla. Flowering commences in late summer to early autumn and blooms still appear as the leaves of the trees begin to fall. *15 × 30*

Geranium 83, 84

These 'Cranesbills' are not the popular half-hardy bedding out plants usually called 'Geraniums' which in fact belong to the genus *Pelargonium* (page **199**). The cranesbills are however a useful group of hardy border or rockery subjects which grow in well-drained soil in sun or part shade. These are plants best seen *en masse* when the clumps form bold groups. The colourful saucer-shaped flowers carried in umbels are displayed over many weeks of the summer months. The low growers are at home on the rock garden; those which spread can be used as ground cover among shrubs. Division is easy when the plants are out of flower. Several kinds self-seed in some soils and may need to be kept in check.

—'Ballerina' is a vigorous hybrid which bears masses of dark-centred lilac-pink flowers for weeks. In our illustration the tiny yellow flowers of *Viola aetolica* have pushed themselves through the dense mat of 'Ballerina' leaves to flower in the sun. *20 × 30*

—*cinereum* **'Apple Blossom'** bears light, clear pink slightly veined flowers on a dense, spreading plant. This is a good choice for the rock garden or edging. *15 × 30*

— — 'Subcaulescens' forms dense mounds of grey-green foliage and stems of fairly large rich carmine-red flowers. *15 × 30*

—*endressii* **'A. T. Johnson'** which is a splendid ground cover plant is a version of 'French cranesbill' with light pink flowers. *40 × 60*

—'Johnson's Blue' is a hybrid with clear blue flowers in upright growth and makes a good border plant. *45 × 40*

—*macrorrhizum* **'Album'** is a

plant which grows best where the soil does not completely dry out in hot weather. The sturdy stems spring from a woody rootstock producing its bunches of white flowers amid large scented leaves. *30 × 45*

—*pratense* **'Plenum'** is the double blue form of the cottage garden 'Meadow cranesbill', a plant which is so useful in the summer border. *45 × 45*

Geum

Geum, or 'Avens', are easily grown perennials for the border, wild garden or rockery depending on species grown. Some are good for cutting their flowers often opening singly on upright branches and appear over many weeks during the summer. Generally planted in the border they are not choosey about soil although they do prefer a moist rather than dry site. These are plants that require frequent lifting, dividing and firmly replanting if they are to be kept growing vigorously. This may be done in fall or spring, remembering to incorporate some humus when preparing the ground. Except when the seeds are purchased named kinds cannot be increased with

any guarantee of success other than in this manner. The seeds can be sown under glass during the spring, pricked off and grown on for planting out during the following summer.

—*chiloense* **'Fire Opal'** usually has semi-double luminous orange-red cup-shaped flowers on sturdy stems. *45 × 30*

——**'Lady Stratheden'** is an older cv still justly popular displaying its semi-double blooms for many weeks. *60 × 45*

——**'Mrs Bradshaw'** bears double bright red flowers, a fine old form. *45 × 45*

—*montanum* is a charming rockery plant from S. Europe with hairy leaves and short stems of clear yellow saucers. *20 × 30*

—*rivale* **'Leonard's Variety'** is an improvement on the British native 'Water avens' with stems of nodding pink flowers produced from tufts of bright green leaves. *30 × 45*

—*x borisii* bears distinctive pale orange flowers which emerge from darker orange buds. Use this low growing, rather spreading plant on the rock garden or at the front of a border. *30 × 50*

Gilia 103
G. × hybrida is the botanical

name for 'Leptosiphon', a much branched annual with slender stems bearing many tiny flowers in shades of yellow, violet and brown. Seed may be sown out of doors in an open sunny situation during the late spring with a further sowing in summer if a continuing display is required. *20 × 15*

Godetia

Hardy annuals, the garden plants being derived from the North American species, *G. amoena* and *G. grandiflora*. These may be sown outside where they are to flower in spring or fall. Godetias are showy plants related to the clarkia's and with similar foliage. The funnel-shaped blooms are carried in erect leafy spikes and may be had in single or double forms. An open sunny position suits them, the most shapely plants will develop where they are well spaced and amply supplied with water during a dry spell.

The many colours available include pink, red, violet and white. Some named cultivars are offered by seedsmen including the lovely 'Sybil Sherwood', salmon pink. *35 × 25* **85**

Gypsophila

These are both annuals and perennials. They are well-loved plants much valued for their blooms produced either in billowing masses or on slender stems. A sunny well-drained bed or border will be required for these. If your soil is not naturally limy a dressing of hydrated lime prior to the initial planting will be of great benefit. Most sorts are suitable for cutting. Annual 'Gyp', as the market traders know it, is very easy to raise from seed sown in a sunny spot.

— *elegans* is an annual with smooth greyish leaves and white or pink flowers carried in panicles. *45 × 30*

— *paniculata* is a useful border plant forming a large mound of many branched stems spangled with tiny white flowers. This long-lived perennial needs a deep soil in order to accommodate the large rootstock. Once positioned the young plants must remain undisturbed. They can be raised from seed or cuttings of small side-shoots rooted in sand during the spring. *90 × 90*

——'**Bristol Fairy**' is a superb double sort normally purchased since these are raised by grafting onto the single sort – a specialist operation. It is sometimes possible to purchase packets of "double" seed about 50% of which come true. *60 × 90*

——'**Rosy Veil**' ('Rosenchleirer') has flowers which are white at first, becoming pink. A pretty sort for cutting. *35 × 90*

—*repens* is a semi-shrubby prostrate alpine with white or pale rose flowers which builds itself up into an extensive mound when well sited on a sunny slope. *20 × 60*

——'**Dorothy Teacher**' is a superior form of the above with prostrate stems of deep sea-green leaves and small clusters of clear pink flowers. *10 × 45* **82**

Helenium 86

In these easily grown border plants the colourful daisy-like blooms each with a large central disc are produced with abandon on stiff, upright leafy stems. Normal garden soil suits the 'Sneezeworts' which may be planted in either full sun or part shade. Mulching in early spring is of course of great benefit. This helps to keep the soil moist for these will show their displeasure of dry conditions by the browning of the lower leaves. The tendency is for clumps to develop a mass of new shoots during the spring. If the number of these is reduced at that time, stronger stems will result. New stock can be procured by dividing clumps up in early spring and, except for the smaller growers, selecting single crowns for growing on. The garden cultivars have been developed largely from the North American *H. autumnale*.

——'**Bruno**' is mahogany-red, late flowering. *90 × 45*

——'**Chipperfield Orange**', orange-yellow, tall and late. *110 × 50*

——'**Coppelia**', coppery-orange. *90 × 45*

——'**Golden Youth**', rich yellow, early. *70 × 40*

——'**Moerheim Beauty**', bronze-red. *90 × 45*

——'**Pumilum Magnificum**', rich yellow. *75 × 40*

——'**Wyndley**', orange-yellow with brown flecks. *60 × 50*

Helianthus

The 'Sunflowers' are a group of annuals and perennials easily grown in light fertile soil. They are normally placed towards the rear of the mixed border because of their height. As their name might suggest a position in the full sun suits them best. Staking of the very large annual sunflowers is advised for although these have massive stems they have also to carry a considerable weight when in flower. For the largest flowers place three seeds where each plant is wanted, later thinning to the one strongest seedling. They require a richer soil than the perennial kinds. The main cultivation requirement for these is to lift them every two or three years, dividing and then replanting in soil to which a little decayed manure and fertilizer has been added. These clumps will be better when supported with strong canes which are lightly tied around with garden string as the plants grow.

—annuus is the common annual sunflower with massive daisy-like flowers frequently as large as dinner plates. Yellow is the predominating colour others are suffused with red. Height varies between *60—300 × 20—60*. Our colour plate shows 'Sungold' a fine double. *75 × 40* **93**

—decapetalus The garden forms of this border perennial have large, rather rough green leaves and strong stems carrying golden-yellow blooms. They also make good cut flowers.

——'Loddon Gold' has large, fully double yellow flowers in abundance. *150 × 45*

——'Maximus' is a selected plant with extra large single yellow blooms. *170 × 45*

Helichrysum

A large genus of annuals, perennials and shrubs few of which are met with in gardens. Of these the best known are the annual 'everlastings' with strawy 'petals' (actually bracts) which remain colourful when dried. All the species require a well-drained sunny spot and the alpines should be planted with a dressing of fine shingle beneath the foliage to ensure good drainage for the woolly leaves. Some of the newer dwarf kinds make a bold show in the annual border (the illustration is of a single flower head of one of these).

—*arenarium* (Yellow everlasting) is a border plant with erect stems of silver leaves topped by a cluster of tiny yellow 'straw' flowers each with an orange centre. Increase these plants by severing the woody rootstock. *30 × 25*

—*bellidioides* has prostrate green stems with silver-backed leaves and bears tiny clusters of white flowers. A choice New Zealand alpine plant for the rockery. *7 × 30*

—*bracteatus* is the familiar annual 'everlasting'. Originally from Australia, these now come in various colours and height ranges. In each the central yellow disc of florets is surrounded by the strawy bracts which are the main feature of dried arrangements. Cut the stems when the flowers are just open and not going over, tie them in a loose bunch before hanging in a cool airy place to dry. Kinds to grow include:

— — 'Tall large-flowered Mixed', these are in red, white, purple and orange etc. *90 × 35*

— — 'Dwarf Double Mixed' are a mixture similar to the above but on more compact little bushes. *45 × 30*

— — 'Hot Bikini' is a striking F_1 hybrid producing its brilliant orange-red flowers on compact bushes. *30 × 25* **87**

Heliopsis

Much like *Helianthus* to which these annuals and perennials are closely related and also from North America. The border plants which we grow are a valuable addition to the garden for their ease of culture and showy flowers. A light fertile soil if provided with generous amounts of compost will produce fine green leaves and sturdy stems. *Heliopsis* are easily increased by division of the roots during early spring. Young plants do not always reach their full height in their first year of transplanting so do not judge these on their initial showing. Slow establishment is one of the reasons that the clumps can remain undisturbed for 3–5 seasons before necessary replanting.

—*scabra* 'Ballet Dancer' bears clear yellow double flowers on erect branching stems. This colour contrasts beautifully with the blue

of *Aconitum* or delphiniums.
90 × 45 **90**

——'Gigantea' has golden yellow single flowers on tall stems.
120 × 60

——'Golden Plume' bears double bright yellow flowers.
90 × 45

——'Patula' has frilled blooms in an orange-yellow shade. *90 × 45*

Helleborus 88

Choice winter, spring and summer flowering plants with attractive deeply divided leaves and stems of large saucer-shaped flowers which are produced either singly or in clusters. These plants are best when placed in groups at the edge of a shrub border in light shade. They resent disturbance so when first planting select young stock and provide them with soil well prepared with old manure or peat and fertiliser. Increase is by division of the crowns in early spring or seeds sown when ripe. Place the pots of seed in a cold frame or a shady position outside. Carefully watch for slugs when the plants are young!

—*lividus corsicus* bears long lasting clusters of pale green flowers during the spring. *40 × 50*

—*niger* (Christmas rose) These have white blooms with a central boss of golden stamens. They open very early in the year and may require protection from the elements. Some strawy litter on a pane of glass supported by wires will help at this time. The flowers last exceptionally well in water.
20 × 40

—*orientalis* (Lenton Rose) Usually offered as mixed seedlings in white, pink or purple these are taller and later flowering than the above. The flowers are in small bunches at the ends of the smooth stems. *30 × 40*

Hemerocallis 92

The 'Day lily' is so called as the flowers (opening individually in succession from the many buds) seldom last longer than a day. Fortunately the buds keep developing and a good display is assured. Many striking new colours have been introduced in recent years which no doubt accounts for their present popularity. The leaves are almost grass-like as they develop from the crowns during the spring and these remain attractive when the plants are out of flower. Day lilies are easily grown on moisture retentive soils and will tolerate a little shade. Division of the crowns is an easy way to increase stock. This should only be undertaken when the plants are overcrowded as it takes some little while for the fleshy roots to re-establish after moving. The following have been developed from *H. fulva.*

——**'Black Magic'** has rich mahogany-red petals with yellow centre. *90 × 45*

——**'Golden Chimes'** has masses of small golden yellow flowers on blackish stems. *60 × 30*

——**'Morocco Red'** is brown-red with yellow centre. *60 × 30*

——**'Pink Damask'**, clear rich pink. *75 × 45*

——**'Stafford'** is a taller grower with deep red petals and yellow centre. *90 × 45*

Heuchera

With no particular soil requirements, all they need is a well-drained spot, 'Coral flower' produces slender stems of tiny bell-like flowers during the summer months. Their evergreen foliage remains neat and individuals form well pro-portioned clumps. You may notice that the crowns have a tendency to push themselves out from the ground, so firm rather deep planting is the way to increase your stock. Seeds will grow but remember that the seedlings will not be true to name and may well be inferior to the parent plant. The splendid hybrids now available which are such an improvement over the old sorts are all the result of crosses made by Alan Bloom of Bressingham Gardens. Plant them in borders or use as an edging. Although the flowering stems can range in height from 50cm to 90cm the foliage remains low forming a mound.

— **'Coral Cloud'** produces masses of light coral pink flowers – good for cutting too!

— **'Firebird'** has sturdy stems of deep red bells.

— **'Greenfinch'** bears flowers of an unusual shade of yellow-green a colour much appreciated by the ladies for their floral arrangements.

——**'Oakington Jewel'** with coral-red flowers contrast well against heavily marbled leaves.

— **'Pearl Drops'** are white with

the merest hint of pink.

— **'Red Spangles'** has sturdy stems which carry wide-mouthed crimson-red bells.

— **'Scintillation'** is a long-flowering plant with each tiny pink bloom rimmed in red.

× *Heucherella*

Plants of this hybrid genus have come about by the crossing of *Heuchera* with the nearly related *Tierella*. Each spring and for several weeks following dainty sprays of delicate pink flowers appear above the dark green, brown marbled leaves. These low growers are useful for ground cover where the soil is freely drained; the best specimens are usually seen where there is light shade to protect the plants during the hottest part of the day. Careful division of the clumps in early spring will furnish a plentiful supply of new planting material.

— × *tiarelloides* produces pale pink flowers which are displayed on tiny stems. This plant, although spreading by means of stolons, does not become invasive under normal conditions. *30 × 60*

——**'Bridget Bloom'** has attractive leaves and dainty sprays of flesh-pink flowers produced over many weeks mark these plants as useful subjects for a shady border.

45 × 45

Hutchinsia

H. alpina is dwarf and spreading, very free with its white flowers. This is a charming little Pyrenean plant which grows best in deep sandy loam. They are quick growing under ideal conditions, our illustration taken in a friend's garden shows a group of three plants from small pots just two months after planting. To increase stock sow seeds or take cuttings after they have flowered and have been lightly trimmed. *20 × 40* **89**

Iberis

These hardy annuals and perennials are easily grown in light well-drained soil, preferably in full sun. Their freely produced, clustered flowers have the typically cross-shaped petals of the Cruciferae and have a delicate fragrance. In mild places seed of the annuals may be sown during late summer for an early display. If sowing is delayed until the spring a later flowering date may be expected. They make fine edging plants, or may be massed in beds. The evergreen species usually seen, of which there are some attractive very slow-growing miniature forms, are shrubby plants which are useful for the fronts of borders or for planting up vertical crevices on the rock garden. Propagation of these is by sowing seeds or taking cuttings of the better plants (and named cultivars) after flowering, rooting them in pots of sand compost placed in a lightly shaded frame.

—*umbellata* (Candytuft) is an annual long grown in gardens, some of the modern colours are very striking compared with those formerly grown. **24**

—— **'Fairy Mixed'** forms neat dome-shaped plants of yellow, pink, white, mauve or rose. *20 × 30*

—— **'Red Flash'** is an even grower with brilliant carmine-red flowers. *30 × 45*

—*sempervirens* is an evergreen species producing masses of pure white flowers during spring and early summer. *25 × 45*

—— **'Little Gem'** forms tiny, neatly mounded bushlets bearing white flowers. *15 × 15*

—— **'Snowflake'** is another rock plant also with white flowers but larger than above. *25 × 30*

Impatiens

These colourful plants consist of both tender perennials and half-hardy annuals; in Europe they are normally treated as the latter and not planted out until all danger of late frost is past. Their stems are very brittle and succulent producing spurred flowers from the leaf axils. The best plants will be found in either sun or part shade where soil does not dry out. Peat or old manure should be added to the soil prior to planting. There are many splendid new sorts that are first class garden plants when massed in beds or window boxes. Propagation is from seeds sown under glass during the spring or cuttings taken during the summer. These root with great ease – even in a jar of water.

—*balsamina* is an erect plant with thick stems and toothed, oval leaves. The flowers are large and showy both single and double in several bright colours: rose, scarlet, white, violet etc. *45 × 30*

—*sultani* these are usually very branched with succulent stems and masses of bright flowers. They need very little covering for the seeds when sown inside.

——'General Guisan' has bright red and white striped blooms. 25 × 30

——Imp strain (F_1 hybrids) is available in single colours or as a mixture and either make fine bedding plants for sun or shade. 25 × 30

——'Minette Mixed' are spreading plants carpeting the ground with a mass of flowers. 15 × 25

Inula 100

The garden-worthy species of this genus are easily grown perennial plants generally forming leafy clumps with stems of rayed or daisy-like flowers. They succeed best in moisture retentive soil in sun or part shade. The Himalayan, *I. royleana* in our photograph bears large yellow flowers for weeks. It was taken in the Pukakura Park, New Plymouth, New Zealand. These plants are readily increased by dividing the clumps before growth commences in the spring. 60 × 75

Iris

The genus *Iris* is a very large one containing both bulbs and plants with rhizomatous roots (stout roots spreading either on or just below the soil surface). The genus is normally divided up into different groups because of the number of species. Of these one of the more important is the Bearded iris, *I. germanica*. These are magnificent hardy border plants with smooth pointed leaves arranged in the form of a fan, showy flowers in a wide range of colours appear from late spring to summer (May/June in Europe). The Flag iris are grouped according to the height of their flowering stems into tall, intermediate and dwarf so that the nurseryman is able to supply plants for almost any border situation. Full sun, good drainage and rich soil containing a certain amount of lime are the points to consider when contemplating a planting of these. The roots require lifting periodically and divided – just after flowering is a good time.

Keep only the best of the outside rhizomes for replanting. The tips of the leaves of the new single crown plant can be trimmed both to reduce transpiration loss and also as an aid to stop the plant rocking in a breeze. When planting ensure that the rhizome is partially exposed on the soil surface. Water these regularly until re-established. 94–97

——'Berkeley Gold' is a clear rich yellow. *100 × 35*

——'Black Swan' is a velvety dark purple-black. *90 × 35*

——'Blue Shimmer' has blue markings on a white flower. *90 × 35*

——'Braithwaite' has lavender standards and maroon falls. *70 × 35*

——'Butterscotch Kiss' is pale orange. *100 × 35*

——'Firecracker' is purple-brown with yellow markings. *100 × 35*

——'Mary Randall' has a bright orange beard which contrasts against the old rose to the petals. *90 × 35*

——'Wabash' has white standards and blue falls. *100 × 35*

—*kaempferi* has beautiful orchid-like blooms which open out nearly flat during the summer. These are often planted in water but they will be found to grow equally well in a moist, lime-free border. *75 × 35*

—*laevigate* 'Rose Queen' is an attractive iris with light pink blooms. The species is adaptable for moist soil or shallow water. *60 × 30*

—*pumila* There are several named plants available of this early-flowering miniature version of the Bearded iris. Use these in the rock garden or front of the border. *10–20 × 20*

—*siberica* is a border or water-side plant. The grassy clumps send up slender, wiry stems bearing small, neat flowers during early summer. These are useful for cutting and the dried seed pods are attractive winter decoration.

——'Perry's Blue' has deep blue flowers. *90 × 25*

——'Snow Queen' is pure white. *90 × 25*

——'Tropic Night' has dark violet blooms. *90 × 25*

Jasione
These are low-growing perennials with leaves in the form of a basal rosette and stems of bright blue flowers in rounded heads. A sandy loam suits them and they can be increased from divisions or seeds sown when ripe.

—*perennis* is a hardy rock plant

from European mountains which forms mats of tufted crowns which bear slender stems of round flower heads in brightest blue. *20 × 25* **91**

Kniphofia 98, 99

These are clump forming, originally South African, perennials which have very long narrow leaves with stout stems supporting their showy inflorescence (Red hot pokers) composed of tiny tubular flowers. They are suitable for border planting or ideally as bold specimens in beds of their own. Some strawy litter placed around the plants with their leaves tied together protecting the crown is a precaution worthwhile in cold areas during the winter months. Their soil requirement is a sandy loam with plenty of very old manure added. Adequate water must be provided in dry weather if the plants are in active growth. Leave the dense clumps undisturbed for as long as possible unless new stock is required. Division of the crowns during the spring is the method used to increase named kinds. Several splendid hybrids have become available in recent years.

— *galpinii* **'Bressingham Comet'** is a fine introduction far better than the species with orange-red flowers and narrow grassy-like leaves. *50 × 45*

— *modesta* was the name on the plant we photographed in the Wisley Gardens. It had flowers of a delightful creamy-white shade. *60 × 60*

— *praecox* **'Winter Cheer'** is an early flowering sort with deep orange flowers. *120 × 60*

— *uvaria* (hybrids and cultivars)

—— **'Alcazar'** is bright orange. *90 × 60*

—— **'C. M. Prichard'** is a strong grower with dark orange flowers. *185 × 60*

—— **'Gold Else'** is an early sort with golden-yellow blooms. *75 × 60*

—— **'Maid of Orleans'** is cream. *90 × 60*

—— **'Royal Standard'** is an older sort with red and yellow bicolour blooms. *90 × 60*

—— **'Samuels Sensation'** has bold spikes of scarlet. *150 × 90*

Lathyrus

This name covers the 'peas',

both culinary and ornamental. In our case we have selected but one for a description, – *L. odoratus*, the familiar 'Sweet pea'. These favorite climbing annual flowers have a long history as garden plants going back to the sending of seeds of the species to Britain from Southern Italy in 1699. Over 150 years were to elapse before any change was to be seen from their typical wild colour – pretty as it is: not until the final quarter of the last century were varieties in a distinct colour range introduced. Gathering momentum, introductions flooded onto the market from that time up to the present day and many thousands of variations have been named. Almost every colour is represented, mostly delicately scented in single and double forms, frilled or waved petals, and short or long stems etc. Cultivation of these delightful flowers consists of thorough preparation of the site with deep digging or trenching adding plenty of organic material. A light dressing of a complete fertiliser should be incorporated into the surface two weeks or so before the young plants are set out. They succeed best where the soil is well-drained but kept moist in dry weather. Seeds may be sown in pots during the fall and either under glass in spring or directly where they are to flower. Mice are very fond of the large seeds and precautions must be taken against these pests (we shake the seeds in a plastic bag which has a few drops of kerosene in it). For quality cut flowers, or exhibiting, the young plants are usually treated as cordons reducing each to a single stem and training them up individual canes. When the tall sorts are required for decorating a border, twenty or more seedlings are set in a circle, perhaps a meter in diameter, placing small twiggy sticks with them. Taller, bushy sticks are later pushed into position to support the flowering plants. Further care includes removing all of the old flowers as they fade. Keep the soil moist (a thorough soak now and then rather than a frequent splash!) and you will have sweet peas to enjoy all summer long.

——'Air Warden' scarlet-cerise.

——'Carlotta' carmine.

——'Elizabeth Taylor' clear mauve.

——'Knee Hi Mixed' are quite unlike the earlier kinds of sweet pea in the fact that when spring sown and planted in the border they require no support making them first rate garden plants. The flowers are very freely borne in a good colour range. *45 × 70*

——'Jet Set Mixed' could be described as an advance on the 'Knee Hi' strain. Similarly they require little or no support and bear good stems of flowers in clear bright shades of blue, mauve, pink and scarlet. *45 × 80* **102**

——'Mrs C. Kay' lavender.

——'Mrs R. Bolton' deep pink.

——'Noel Sutton' blue.

——'Radar' salmon.

——'Reconnaissance' cream edged with pink

——Spencer mixture. These are the familiar large flowered strain frequently sold as named cultivars. (see below).

——'Swan Lake' pure white.

Lavatera

These are a mixed group of plants including shrubs as well as annuals and herbaceous subjects. The 'Tree mallow' described, although shrubby, is better when treated as a her-baceous plant, as it is normally in Britain, cutting the stems back to within 15cm of the soil each spring.

—*olbia* 'Rosea' ('Tree mallow', or 'Tree lavatera') has wide clear pink flowers well displayed against its grey, rather hairy foliage. Plant these very large growers singly to fill a large space in the border. A sunny, dry, well-drained place should be chosen and when growing well you will be rewarded with a long succession of flowers. Cuttings of new basal shoots will root if placed in a heated frame or greenhouse; seeds may also be tried. *120 × 90*

—*trimestris* is an annual mallow originally from the mediterranean area. During the summer it bears masses of very pretty, clear pink, open, trumpet-shaped blooms on branched, upright stems. These are hardy plants and may be sown *in situ* where a moderate to tall subject is needed. In most gardens staking with bushy peasticks will probably be required as a pre-caution against the plants blowing over. *90 × 60* **104**

185

Lewisia

L. howellii is a choice rock plant suited to positioning in a dry stone wall or well-drained rock bed. A native of Oregon, United States, this species forms rosettes of narrow, flat, wavy-edged leaves and has short stems of deep flowers. Increase is by division of the crowns in early summer or from seeds sown when ripe. Hybrids are frequent when the latter method is chosen to propagate stock. These are welcome in the garden for the fine flowers they often produce. Young stock is best over-wintered in a cold frame in damp countries such as Britain to minimise the risk of the fleshy leaved crowns rotting off. *15 × 20* **148**

Ligularia

The garden plants selected from this genus of 80 or so species have handsome leaves and bold flower spikes. Moisture retentive soil well enriched with decayed vegetable matter is essential for their well-being, any hint of dryness resulting in wilting leaves.. With these requirements met, they are easily grown plants, perfect for the larger border, light woodland and particularly good for massing at the edge of a pool or lake. Propagation is by dividing the crowns in spring.

— *clivorum* 'Desdemona'. Derived from the original Chinese species this plant has large rounded purple leaves with bright orange flowers displayed on branched spikes. *120 × 60*

—— 'Greynog Gold' also has the typical round leaves this time with bronze-centred golden yellow flowers. *90 × 45*

— *stenocephala* 'The Rocket' is a striking plant when seen *en masse* with its towering spikes of slender black stems festooned with small pale yellow blooms. This plant was formerly known (and sometimes still listed as) *Senecio przewalskii* which has now fortunately been changed to something more pronounceable! *150 × 90* **101**

Linum

The 'Flax's' are dainty border, showy annuals and rock plants suited to warm positions in almost any well-drained soil. The perennial kinds can be increased from seeds or cuttings of firm shoots placed in a frame during the spring. Seeds of the annuals may be sown where they are to flower when the soil becomes dry and warm after the winter.

— *arboreum* forms a grey-green bushlet with short stems of clustered clear yellow flowers in late spring. These are charming little plants for the rock garden or border. *30 × 40*

— *flavum* has similar style flowers to the above, perhaps a little more golden, on erect arching leafy green stems for most of the summer. *25 × 35*

— *grandiflorum* is a very free-flowering annual originally from North Africa. The wide, funnel-shape blooms are carried in clusters and come in shades of bright crimson, blue and white. *45 × 30*

— *narbonense* has tall, very slender stems with clusters of surprisingly large pale blue flowers during the summer. Divide their roots regularly to maintain vigour. *45 × 25*

— *salsoloides* is an attractive rock plant which smothers itself with open, white flowers. *10 × 20*

Lobelia 131

The dwarf growing blue lobelias included in this very large group are very popular edging plants for summer beds. Although really perennial these are usually raised annually. The taller late summer-flowering sorts, described briefly below, although not reliably hardy in colder countries are frequently planted out permanently in borders or by the waterside.

— *cardinalis* 'Queen Victoria' The tall leafy stems of this fine hybrid are deep purple-red in colour and the flowers which are carried in terminal racemes bright scarlet. In cold places a winter covering of dead leaves, straw or bracken is advisable. Remove this in the spring as the blackish-purple new shoots are emerging. When about 5cm high will be the time to select cuttings of these to increase your stock of plants. Root these in sandy compost under glass. In most soils it should be possible to detach a few rooted crowns which can be replanted where they are to remain. *90 × 30*

— *erinus* The dwarf blue lobelia are one of the more frequently planted of summer flowering half-hardy annuals. The compact forms are mostly used for edging beds, the trailers in pots, baskets and planters. Their seeds are very fine and barely need covering when thinly sown in boxes of light compost. As growth is comparatively slow, an early start in the new year is essential for these. When the seed has germinated well, prick the seedlings out in tiny patches of 4 or 5 for they are too small to separate. Finally harden them off and delay planting until frost is past.

—— **'Blue Cascade'** has light blue cascading flowers. *7 × 25*

—— **'Cambridge Blue'** is a neat grower producing masses of light blue flowers. *15 × 20*

—— **'Crystal Palace'** has dark leaves and bears deep blue flowers. *15 × 20*

—— **'Mrs Clibran'** is voilet-blue each small bloom with a white eye. *15 × 20*

Lupinus
Hybrids of **L. polyphyllus** (lupin) are popular perennial border plants due to their quick growth and tall spikes of evenly spaced blooms. Lupins grow best in a light, well drained soil dressed with peat and bone meal before planting. A position in sun or light shade may be selected. Seeds sown outside in midsummer will develop into fine young plants of a suitable size for transplanting during the following spring. *90 × 45* **106**

Lythrum
The 'Purple loosetrifes' are European natives which are invaluable for moist soil although normal situations are tolerated. Flowers are produced during the summer on upright bushy growth. It is worth removing blooms as they fade for more will follow. Lift and divide these plants regularly when they are dormant.

—**virgatum** 'The Rocket' has rose flowers in dainty spikes. *110 × 60*

Malva
M. alcea is a 'Mallow' which is easily grown and long-lived in poor, dry soil. Its branched stems clad rather sparsely with deeply lobed, toothed leaves, bear stems of pale rose-purple flowers in long succession. *150 × 60*

Matricaria
(*M. eximia* is correctly *Chrysanthemum parthenium*) Treat the double flowered 'Golden Ball' and 'Silver Ball' as half-hardy annuals trans-

planting them into light soil in full sun. Here they will develop into little bushes studded all summer with small button-like blooms. *20 × 25*

Mattiola

More familiarly known as 'Stocks' these are long standing favourites with gardeners everywhere. Easily raised from seed they have all the attributes of fine garden flowers namely: attractive grey foliage, free blooming, bearing single and double flowers in pleasing colours together with delightful, clove-like scent. The plants are generally neat and compact or should we say 'stocky'? For this was how their common name was originally derived. The stocks of today were formerly Stock-gilliflowers, wallflowers used to be gilliflowers and carnations were Clove-gilliflowers in years past. The plants that we grow have been derived from *M. incana* a single flowered European species. The two main groups are the summer stocks (annuals) and winter stocks (biennials). There are, in addition, many divisions within each of these two main types. The most frequently seen of the summer group are the ten-week stocks so named on account of the fact that they flower in ten weeks from a spring sowing. Some biennial sorts are: Brompton, Intermediate or East Lothian strain. Seed of the above should be sown in trays under glass (beware of damping-off at this stage), pricked out when large enough to handle before being finally planted out. All stocks are better when grown in a sunny position in rich, preferably alkaline soil. Tall growers may each need a light cane for support and if faded blooms are removed a continued display will result. In cold areas the Brompton stocks can be lifted, wintered under glass and replanted outside again in the spring. As well as the large-flowered kinds another favourite is:

—bicornis (night-scented stock) is easily raised by sowing the seeds in sun or light shade. The single lilac flowers are gloriously scented in the evening but the plants have half-closed blooms during the day. One can hide these by mixing in some seeds of the species below. *35 × 25*

189

Malcomia

M.maritima, or Virginian stocks, have gay little flowers in yellow, pink and blue. They are one of the easiest of all annuals to raise and a favourite for children's gardens. Sow in several batches for continuity. *20 × 15*

Meconopsis 110

The name *Meconopsis* is derived from *mekon* – poppy, and *opsis* – like. When flowering it is not difficult to see the resemblance to their near relatives. It is the colour however of the startling blue-flowered species that must be unique amongst plants. The culture of many of these can be rather taxing especially during the winter months when wet and insect pests take their toll. Our illustration comes from the Savill Garden, the Great Park, Windsor where several species are extremely well grown in a semi-woodland situation. The garden is attractive at all times but, to us, especially so in late spring when the *Meconopsis* and *Primulas* are looking their best. Generally speaking a moisture retaining yet free drained, leafy, acid soil is best for these plants. Too much moisture around the base of the rosette of leaves must be avoided for many fine plants are lost during the winter months by 'crown rot'. Part shade tends to prolong the life of the short-lived blooms. Seeds sown as ripe in pots of sand, loam and peat should germinate well. Seedlings must be pricked out into boxes of a similar mix and kept under cover during the winter.

— *baileyii* (*betonicifolia*) is the justly famous 'Himalayan blue poppy'. Their clear blue flowers with central boss of golden stamens will appear after their second year from seed. If allowed to flower at that time the plants frequently die. For this reason many prefer to remove buds as they first appear being content with the attractive crowns of orange bristly leaves until a stout plant is built up. *90 × 30*

— *quintuplinervia* (Harebell poppy) has soft lavender-blue nodding bells often carried singly at the tops of the stems this is normally a reliable perennial. *30 × 25*

— × *sheldonii* (*betonicifolia × grandis*) is a superb seldom seen hybrid. *75 × 30* **108**

Mesembryanthemum

M. criniflorum (Livingstone daisy) is a mat forming half-hardy annual from South Africa with green leaves glistening with white glands. The masses of brilliantly coloured daisy-like flowers remain closed when dull but open up again in sunlight. Seeds are usually raised under glass for planting out at the edges of borders or to fill spaces in the rockery. Dry, well-drained sunny positions in almost any type of soil will ensure a fine display. *10 × 30* **III**

Mimulus 113

'Monkey flower', or 'Monkey musk', are showy plants with rather fleshy stems and leaves. They are suited to moist positions in the border, rock garden or near water. In addition to soil moisture they appreciate a sheltered spot in which to display their masses of comparatively large flowers. Although perennial seed-raised strains are often treated as half-hardy annuals, the shoots of all root readily if cut from low on the plant, perhaps with a little amount of root already present. Set these in

moist soil where they are to remain.

— × *burnetii* bears masses of orange-brown flowers. *25 × 30*

— *cupreus* The cultivars of this species are extremely bright and free flowering, generally more dwarf than the others.

— — 'Scarlet Bee' has flame-red blooms. *15 × 25*

— — 'Whitecroft Scarlet' is vermilion-red. *15 × 25*

— *luteus* 'A.T. Johnson' has large, deep yellow, gloxinia-like flowers well spotted and blotched with reddish-brown. *40 × 30*

Monarda 116

Cultivars of *M. didyma* (Bergamot) which are described below are hardy, clump-forming plants with upright stems bearing large mint-like, perfumed leaves. The whorls of flowers which include brightly coloured bracts are carried in dense terminal heads. The species is a native of N. America where in nature it forms large patches. This gives us a clue as to how it looks best in the border or by the streamside. Prepared soil which never really dries out completely is best for these; mulching the soil each spring will help to conserve moisture in dryer soils. Division of the criss-cross dormant roots will provide new planting material. These plants are among those that require frequent division to keep them growing vigorously. Kinds to grow include:

— — 'Cambridge Scarlet' which is an older favourite with scarlet flowers. *90 × 60* **112**

— — 'Croftway Pink' has bunches of clear pink flowers and the scented foliage of the group. *90 × 60*

— — 'Prairie Night' bears unique violet-purple flowerheads. *90 × 60*

— — 'Snow Maiden' is a rather less vigorous pure white form. *75 × 55*

Myosotis

The 'Forget-me-Nots' are a large group of low growing annuals and short lived perennials including some choice, seldom seen alpines. More familiar are the ever popular blue bedding plants so much part of the spring garden in Britain. These are moderately tolerant of light shade although sun seems to suit them better. A sandy soil that does not dry out too quickly when the days warm up after winter is ideal. Although almost invariably seen as ground cover under tulips or other spring bulbs there are other uses: try them in a rock garden group, in window boxes or tubs, by the waterside. (*M. scorpioides* is a British native found naturally near water). The plants listed below are perennial although in some soils their life is a short one. They can be increased by rooting cuttings of green leafy shoots but raising them all from seed is more usual. Most gardeners treat the bedding plants as biennial by sowing the seeds in a moist border during the late spring. At one time we used to spread the lifted plants in a spare corner of the kitchen garden when their flowers were over and were rewarded with an ample supply of young seedlings. After an initial transplanting the young clumps are set out during the fall where they are to flower.

—*alpestris* is the parent of the dwarf garden cultivars.

—— **'Blue Ball'** is the baby of the group which forms compact domes of surprisingly deep blue flowers. *15 × 20*

—— **'Royal Blue'** has rich blue flowers and is a vigorous kind for borders. *30 × 30*

—— **'Ultramarine'** has the tiny clear blue flowers of the group produced above the linear dark green leaves. *20 × 20*

Myosotidium

M. hortensia is the single member of the genus. A native of the Chatham Is. it is a rare garden plant, not too easy to cultivate. It likes a cool, sheltered and moist spot, exactly the conditions found in the Opahihi Botanical Reserve, Taupo, New Zealand where we saw and photographed them. The plants have large, rounded, fleshy leaves and bold corymbs of white edged, light blue flowers during the spring. Propagation is from seed. *40 × 45* **109**

Nasturtium

The popular annual nasturtiums were derived from *Tropaeoleum majus*, plants originally introduced from Peru. There are two main groups: climbing and bush forms. The climbers are rapid growing in poor soil and are therefore invaluable for scrambling over banks and tree stumps. They soon cover an ugly fence with long stems bearing round leaves and bright flowers. The dwarf plants make a fine show in dry soil either in the sun or partial shade. Modern sorts carry masses of colourful, funnel-shaped, generally spurred flowers well above the foliage. Today there are nasturtiums offered by seedsmen with single, semi-double and double blooms. Sow the seeds out-of doors where they are to flower. Young plants will move well if they are lifted with a ball of soil. Kinds to grow include:

—— **'Golden Gleam'** yellow. *40 × 50*

—— **'Red Roulette'**, light red. *40 × 50* **119**

—— **'Scarlet Gleam'** red. *40 × 50*

—— **'Tom Thumb'** dwarf in mixed colours. *20 × 25*

—— **'Whirly bird'**, a spurless mixture. *30 × 35*

Nemesia

Originally from South Africa, these are colourful annuals fine for bedding out and for filling the odd space in the border. They have rather soft, succulent leaves and short terminal racemes of large, funnel-shaped blooms often with a colour contrast in the throat. Treat them as half-hardy annuals if you are raising early plants under glass, or sow the light papery seeds out of doors in a warm, well-drained spot when conditions permit. The established plants are almost hardy and in parts of New Zealand over-wintered out-of-doors ready for a very early display. Kinds to grow include the following cultivars of *N. strumosa*:

— — **'Blue Bird'** is dwarf, even growth with azure flowers. *20 × 20*

— — **'Carnival'** is a bright mixture of reds, cream and yellow. *20 × 20* **137**

— — **'Sparklers'** form dome-shaped plants smothered in multi-hued blooms. *20 × 20*

Nemophila

N. menziesii (Baby blue eyes) is an attractive low-growing hardy annual (*N. insignis* of the seedsmen). Originally natives of North America the low, spreading stems clad with rather hairy leaves bear comparatively large, upturned dish-shaped, sky-blue flowers. For an early display seeds should be sown in fertile garden soil during the fall or later in the spring to flower during the summer months. If the position is to their liking and not too dry they will possibly re-sow themselves. *15 × 20*

Nepeta

Although long known as *N. mussinii* the familiar garden 'Catmint' is now more correctly called *N × faassenii*. This hybrid is a superb edging plant for sunny well-drained soils with its grey leaves and blue flowers rivalling the dwarf forms of lavender for this purpose. Use them along the edge of a drive or perhaps around a rose bed for red or pink roses with the pale lavender-blue spikes of the *Nepeta* must be one of the finest colour combinations one could wish for in the garden. Although their flowers are produced in succession the little grey bushes are attractive even when out of flower. As they do not set, seed increase must be from divisions of the plants or tiny basal cuttings taken in spring. The latter root readily when placed in sandy compost under a cold frame. *30 × 45*

— × *faassenii* '**Superba**' a more robust grower reaching almost three times the size of the normal plant. These may well require supporting with light pea sticks as they tend to become top-heavy in rich soils.

Nicotiana

For evening fragrance there are few flowers to compare with *N. affinis* and its hybrids. Commonly known as 'Tobacco plants' they form tall, open branched bushes with their petunia-like flowers opening in late afternoon and evening. Newer kinds grown today are derived from crosses between *N. affinis* and the hybrid *N. × sanderae*. These range in height from 25–75cm. according to kind selected. Unlike *N. affinis* these hybrids remain open during the day although scent is not as strong

as in the original species. For perfection, tobacco plants should be grown in a warm, sunny position. They have a preference for rich soil and under ideal conditions be prepared to stake the taller sorts. Seedlings are normally raised under glass for planting out later.

—*affinis* (*N. alata grandiflora*) is the original plant from Brazil which has rather dull white flowers but exquisite fragrance. *90 × 60*

— '**Affinis Hybrids**' come in a wide colour range: white, pink, lilac, mauve etc. Most of these plants are evening scented. *90 × 60*

— '**Lime Green**' has as its name suggests pale lime-green flowers. *75 × 40*

— '**Crimson Rock**' is dwarf, very free flowering over an extended period. The masses of crimson blooms remain open during the day. Our illustration taken in the Royal Horticultural Society's Wisley Garden shows these plants bedded out with 'dot' plants of *Ricinus*, the 'Castor oil plant'. *45 × 30* **121**

Nigella

These hardy annuals popularly known as 'Love-in-the-mist' have erect well-branched stems with leaves cut into fine, feathery segments. The flowers which are set into the top of the bushlet are blue, white or rose. These are useful for cutting and we have also seen the dried pods used for winter decoration. Any soil seems to suit them although they are probably better where it is well drained and sunny. Sow the seeds outside during the fall, thinning and transplanting the seedling in the spring following. Seeds may also be sown during the spring if so desired.

—*damascena* **'Miss Jekyll'** has sky blue semi-double flowers. *30 × 45*

——**'Persian Jewels'** is a mixture of all the colours available. *30 × 45*

Oenothera
A group of rather shrubby perennial plants with striking, wide funnel-shaped blooms produced over a long season. A well-drained soil is best for these. Here they should receive a mulch each spring and water when the site gets hot and the soil dusty. Full sun or light shade suits the border plants. Propagation is from divisions of the fleshy roots in spring. Ensure that these are planted up in a well-drained place for if wet there is a danger that the damaged roots could rot off causing severe damage to the new plant.

—**'Fireworks'** has leafy stems of rather dark foliage, towards the top these are set with long red buds which split to display rich, satiny yellow flowers. *45 × 30*

—**'Highlight'** ('Hoheslicht') is a fine border plant displaying its wide saucer-shaped yellow flowers for weeks on end. *60 × 45*

—*missouriensis* has huge clear yellow blooms which open from the red spotted buds in the evening. These are produced on spreading almost prostrate stems. A spectacular plant for the sunny rock garden or well drained bed. *25 × 45*

Onosma
O. albo-rosea is an attractive spring flowering rock plant from Asia Minor with rather rough hairy leaves and upright stems bent at their ends with one-sided racemes of hanging tubular flowers. These open

white and become pink as they age. These dwarf evergreens delight in exposure to the full sun where their long woody roots can penetrate beneath a cool rock. Our picture was taken in the rock garden in Kew Botanical Garden where a fine selection of choice alpines growing in natural surroundings may be seen at almost any time of the year. Propagation of this *Onosma* is normally from seed although cuttings could be tried. Here there is the problem of watering for the leaves rot off quickly under damp, humid conditions. *25 × 20* **123**

Oxalis

This is a name to strike terror into the hearts of many a gardener with warmer soils for they have encountered the dreaded *O. repens, O corniculata* and *O. pes-caprea* some of the worst weeds there are. The two species described below are non-rampant and can be recommended where a fine show of colour is needed in the sunny rock garden. They are incidentally, also related to the British 'Wood-sorrel' (also called Shamrock) a favourite wild flower. Those listed below need a well-drained sandy loam with the addition of a little moist peat at planting time. The mass of almost stemless, upturned, bell-like flowers open wide on sunny days almost hiding the attractive greyish leaves. These are composed of many leaflets arranged rosette fashion at the ends of the stems. Increase is by division during the spring.

—adenophylla From Chile. The lilac-pink flowers and crinkled grey leaves arise from a bulb-like base. *7 × 15*

—enneaphylla From the Falkland Islands. This has fan-like silvery grey leaves with upturned chalice-shaped white flowers. *7 × 15*

Paeonia

These are noble, long-lived garden flowers with attractive leaves and generally huge, bowl-like blooms now available in a wide colour range. Although it could take up to three seasons after planting for these to appear, the culture of these beautiful flowers is not at all difficult when their requirements are considered. The most important of these is to see that once they are planted they remain undisturbed for many seasons – a separate bed for them is the ideal arrangement. Deep, fertile, neutral to slightly alkaline soil suits them best. This must be well cultivated with plenty of well-rooted manure or compost added for feeding and moisture retention. A dressing of fertiliser can also be given as well as an annual mulch over the crowns. When first planting, the crowns should be no deeper than 3cm below the soil surface. For spacing allow approximately 3 plants per M^2 (2 per sq yd). Propagation is by division of the tuberous roots but for obvious reason this is only undertaken when essential.

—*lactiflora* ('Chinese paeony'). These are available in a wide range of glorious colours and forms. *75 × 60* **124**

——'**Bowl of Beauty**' has a centre of golden stamens to the semi-double pink flower.

——'**Festiva Maxima**' is fully double, white flecked and tipped with carmine.

——'**President Roosevelt**' is red and combines sweet perfume with early flowering.

——'**Sarah Bernhardt**' is of perfect form with the large clear pink blooms held stiffly erect on strong stems.

——'**William Cranfield**' displays single blooms of red petals with golden stamens prominent.

—*officinalis* is the old fashioned cottage garden paeony with double red flowers. Our photo was actually taken in the cottage garden of our former neighbour in Gloucestershire, U.K. *60 × 60* **122**

Papaver

The 'Poppies' are a familiar group of annual and perennial plants. Deep sandy loam suits the large growing *P. orientale* best. Here, each summer their large cup-shaped flowers are produced amidst the bold, hairy leaves. They always make a fine show whether planted singly or in groups. One drawback to these as border plants is the large gap the plants leave after flowering is completed for the season. Propagation of the large growers is by division every few years and root cuttings (see page 41). These should be taken in the winter months and placed in sandy loam for growth to sprout. The colourful annual sorts grow well in a wide range of soils including chalk. Seeds may be sown in patches here and there in the sunniest part of the garden thinning the seedlings out later. In mild areas with well-drained soil the seeds may be sown where the plants are to flower during the autumn and thinned the following spring.

—*alpinum* is a small grower from the Alps with white or yellow flowers. The rock garden is the place for this tiny perennial which often cheekily seeds itself into the most unlikely crannies – especially gravel paths. *15 × 10*

—*nudicaule* is the 'Iceland poppy' which now comes in a variety of colours: white, red, yellow, orange and pink. These are perennials which form tufts of leaves from which the tall flowering stems arise. Their flowers are particularly good for cutting if picked in bud and have their lower stems scalded in boiling water. *30 × 25*

—*orientale* ('Oriental poppies') are the large border plants with such cultivars as:

——'Goliath' which has crimson-red flowers on stiffly erect stems. *90 × 75*

——'Mrs Perry' is salmon-pink with dark blotches at the base of the petals. *90 × 60*

——'Perry's White' has white flowers which contrast well with stronger colours. *90 × 60*

—*rhoeas* ('Corn poppy') is a parent of most of the named strains of annual poppies seen in gardens including the single and double 'Shirley poppies'. The pretty and aptly named 'Ladybird' also belongs to this species. *35 × 25* **118**

—*somniferum* ('Opium poppy') is an easily raised tall annual with smooth grey foliage and stems. The large flowers are available in single, double and frilled forms. *90 × 30* **128**

Pelargonium 129, 132
This name covers the colourful 'Geraniums' of which according to the Royal Horticultural Society's *Dictionary of Gardening* there are between 4 – 5000 named species hybrids and cultivars in cultivation today. The popular name covers not only Zonal pelargoniums but also Ivy-leaved, Miniature and Regal or Show pelargoniums. The latter are not often used in the garden in Europe being more

suited to inside display. Of the first three there is a great choice of colour and form and these are amongst the finest bedding plants that there are. Although tough enough once established they do not survive too much frost especially when newly planted out from a warm greenhouse. Take special care with the hardening off process with these as they have very soft leaves and stems. Once planted out they tolerate dry periods well but will be better if moist peat is well worked into the bed before setting them out. Removing the spent flowers as they go over prolongs their flowering considerably. Due to the problems of overwintering plants inside, most people prefer to purchase young plants anew each season. For anyone wishing to maintain their own stock it is a simple matter to root small tip cuttings in late summer. After potting these on into small pots they may be placed in a sunny window. Keep the compost in the pots on the dry side – not too much heat, and of course no frost.

Recently some fine F_1 hybrid strains of seed-raised plants have been introduced. When sown early in the season good sized flowering specimens may be had in time for summer bedding out. Commercial growers are forecasting that these plants being cheaper to produce when compared to those grown from cuttings may eventually oust the other named sorts as bedding plants from nurseries.

— **'Sprinter'** is another seed-raised kind with many stems of bright scarlet flowers on compact plants. 35×30

Some other named sorts suitable for bedding are:

— **'Carefree'** is a fine strain of these newer geraniums. These F_1 hybrids come in a complete range of separate colours. 35×30

— **'Cal'** is a fine U.S. introduction with large soft pink flowers.

— **'Caroline Schmidt'** has variegated green and yellow leaves and red flowers.

— **'Gustav Emich'** has striking vermilion blooms.

— **'Irene'** bears its red flowers in good sized clusters.

— **'King of Denmark'** is an old favourite with semi-double salmon-pink flowers.

— **'Abel Carriere'** is a quick grower with purple flowers.

— **'Galilee'** has rose-pink flowers and is good for bedding out.

— **'Millfield Gem'** which is a hybrid between Ivy-leaved and Zonal geraniums has fuchsia-purple flowers each with a darker purple blotch.

— **'Mme Crousse'** is a popular large-flowered sort with pale purple-pink blooms.

— **'Mrs Henry Cox'** has a fascinating medley of leaf colours with zonings of black, cream, red and green with orange flowers.

— **'Orangesonne'** was bred in Switzerland. It is a vigorous plant with large heads of clear orange flowers.

— **'Paul Crampel'** although introduced at the end of the last century this bright red-flowered bedder is still the best known today.

— **'Penny'** has semi-double pink flowers and is one of the best of the newer sorts.

— **'Queen of the White's'** is the popular white cultivar. The above are variable, approx. *30 × 35*

Some Ivy-leaved geraniums which have generally more trailing stems and are popular for hanging baskets include:

Peltiphyllum 142

These are bold foliage plants with their large rounded leaves carried at the ends of tall unbranched stalks. The flowering stems grow from stout creeping rhizomes early in the spring and attain almost 1m before uncurling to reveal the dense mass of starry flowers that are arranged in a flat corymb. It is not until sometime after these begin to fade that the leaves appear and it is a strange sight to see bare unbranched flower stems springing haphazardly from the mud in which the plants luxuriate. They can be planted singly or in groups to stabilise a stream bank but wherever they are placed it must be moist for these are bog plants in their native California. Sun or shade suits them equally well. New stock can be obtained by cutting off a crown complete with some roots early in the new year.

— *peltatum* 'Parasol Plant' The species described above bears pale pink flowers in spring. *100 × 100*

Penstemon 134

The garden hybrid penstemons, or 'Beard tongue',

are rather short-lived, semi-evergreen perennials. They are best regarded as half-hardy plants in cold areas raising fresh plants from seed or cuttings each year and over-wintering the stock plants in a cold greenhouse. The garden hybrids are called *P.* × *gloxinoides* no doubt because of the similar flower shape and bright colouring to the exotic glass-house gloxinias. Penstemons are plants for well-drained, warm, protected parts of the garden. Try to mulch around the crowns with compost each spring and keep the soil moist when the plants are in active growth.

— × *gloxinoides*. The garden penstemons have large open-mouthed flowers in several bright colours. *60 × 25*

—— 'Cherry Ripe' bright red.

—— 'Garnet' deep red.

—— 'Sour Grapes' slate blue.

Petunia 131

The petunias we grow today are extremely showy bedding plants. These have been developed over very many years by seedsmen so that now, as well as having single flowers, they come in semi-double and double forms in a wide range of attractive colours. The funnel-shaped blooms are carried in profusion right through the summer. The seed is very small and needs no covering when sown in boxes under glass in early spring. Prick out the seedlings before they become crowded, giving them plenty of light at this stage as there is a tendency for them to become drawn. We prefer to pot-on into peat pots so that when planted out later they receive no check and begin their flowering season right from the start. Soil should be free-draining and, although petunias appreciate humus in the soil, fresh manure or artificials should not be used if too much leafy growth is to be avoided. As well as making fine bedding plants petunias can also be used in baskets and window boxes. *See* Plate showing these growing in a window box outside our friends' Welsh cottage. There are a bewildering number of sorts to choose from. When making a selection remember that the very large-flowered kinds are more prone to rain damage and also need supporting. Some variations of *P.* × *hybrida* are:

—'**Astro**' are sturdy plants with striped red and white flowers. *30 × 35*

— '**Colour Parade**' is a fine mixture of single flowers in a wide range of colour. *20 × 35*

—'**Double Circus**' is a salmon-pink and white bicolour double. Splendid for pots or window boxes. *25 × 30*

— '**Tango**' is a deep scarlet of the 'Grandiflora' type, one of the best for bedding with large waved blooms. *30 × 35*

— '**Double Victorious Mixed**' are dwarf, compact growers with large, double frilled flowers in a wide range of colours including: rose, violet, purple as well as bicolours. *30 × 35*

Phacelia 117
P. campanularia forms a well-branched compact little plant with upright stems of brilliant blue, open-mouthed bell-like flowers. Use these hardy annuals as edging plants or on the rock garden. Seed may be sown in normal garden soil during the spring in either sun or part shade. In mild places a fall sowing can be tried for an early display. *25 × 15*

Phlox
The three groups of *Phlox* normally grown in gardens are the annuals, alpines and border phlox. Given the correct conditions all are of easy culture and comprise some of the showiest plants we have. Seeds of the annual species *P. drummondii* should be sown in gentle heat during mid-spring. Prick out the seedlings later pinching out their growing tips when large enough to make them bush earlier. Very little heat is required for these and they may be safely planted out as soon as they are hardened off in late spring. They can be used as an edging or in groups in the border. The plants in our illustration came from a packet labelled 'Giant Tetra Mixed' which grew to 35cm **138**

——'**Beauty Mixed**' are in a wide colour range produced on compact bushes. *18 × 25*

—— '**Twinkles**' also dwarf, feature star-like centres. *20 × 25*

Some of the many free-flowering dwarf phlox suitable for the rock garden are:

—*amoena* is an attractive dwarf species with heads of rose-purple flowers. *20 × 25*

—*divaricata* 'Chattahoochee', an Eastern North American plant which has stoloniferous roots which each spring produce ascending stems of lavender flowers each with a red eye. *25 × 30* **140**

More mat-forming are the following, all increased by cuttings.˙

—*douglasii* 'Rosea' has tufted, rather congested stems studded with delicate pale rose flowers. *8 × 20*

—*subulata* (Moss phlox) has numerous stems bearing sheets of flowers. *15 × 25* **11, 135, 136**

——'Alexander's Surprise' is an American cultivar with bright pink flowers.

——'Crackerjack' has intense deep red blooms – one of the most striking colours to be seen in late spring flowering rock plants.

——'G. F. Wilson' is a useful contrast colour – pale grey-blue.

For sheer colour the Border phlox are one of the best species for the summer garden. Not all of these flower at the same time so for continuity a selection of cultivars should be planted. These should be placed in groups in good soil which never becomes parched. Indeed the opposite is better for they are tolerant of quite heavy wet soil. Replacement planting should be considered every 3–4 years for older plants tend to deteriorate after that. Each year it is advisable to thin the shoots when they are a few centimetres high leaving the stronger to develop and bear the flowers. Propagation is from cuttings of young shoots which root reasonably well if placed under a cold light. Dividing the crowns in spring retaining only the best portions is also possible as is the 'sowing' of root cuttings. These are taken in early spring from a lifted plant and laid in a box of sandy compost in warmth. Consult a nurseryman's catalogue for a list of up-to-date cultivars. A few of those which we have grown include the following kinds of *P. × hortorum* and *P. paniculata*.

——'Brigadier' has panicles of bright orange-red flowers.

——'**Hampton Court**' produces dark leaves and almost blue flowers. 75 × 38 **134**

——'**Harlequin**' is a distinctive cultivar raised in the Bressingham Gardens. Its leaves are variegated cream and green which make a pleasing foil to the bright purple blooms. 90 × 38

——'**Mount Fujiyama**' bears enormous heads of pure white. 75 × 38

——'**Prince of Orange**' is a vigorous grower with almost luminous orange-red flower trusses. 90 × 38

——'**Sweetheart**' has light red flowers each with a white 'eye'. 75 × 38

Platycodon

This is a monotypic genus from China and Japan, its single member being a most attractive border plant thriving under ordinary conditions. The annual growth is produced from an underground crown, the stems erect and leafy. The inflated flower buds develop near the tops of the shoots. The botanical Latin name of these plants is composed of the words *platys* –

wide, and *kodon* – a bell. When they bloom it is easy to understand the reasoning behind their name for the large buds open up into a broad bell-shaped flower. Propagation is from seed or division of the nobbly roots in early spring. We prefer the latter method as most divisions will be large enough to plant straight out and usually flower the same year. Another reason is that some of the seedlings produce taller specimens than the named cultivars and this is a disadvantage in this group of plants.

—*grandiflorum* '**Mariesii**' is a fine dwarf form of the species with wide open blue flowers. 30 × 40

——'**Mother of Pearl**' has pale pink single blooms. 45 × 30

——'**Snowflake**' is a semi-double pure white. Unusual and worth searching for. 45 × 30

Polygonum 150

A large group of plants, some of which are weeds. Those described below do not however come into this class but will be found to be useful garden subjects. They grow well in ordinary soil although repaying better treatment with more generous growth and ample flowers. Division of the crowns when dormant will furnish additional planting material if required.

—*affine* 'Darjeeling Red' is a splendid version of the original Nepalese species. It is a mat-forming plant with dark green leaves which assume rusty tints in the winter. The deep pink poker-like flowers are produced for weeks. *25 × 45*

——'Donald Lowndes' is a plant that loves to hang down over rock faces in wide carpets of growth. The pale pink flowers are freely borne over a long period. *25 × 45*

—*amplexicaule* 'Speciosum' is best in a moist spot where it forms a bush bearing heart-shaped leaf and rich red flowers for weeks. *120 × 90*

—*bistorta* 'Superbum' ('Bis-tort' or 'Snakewood') is most effective when planted near water a natural home for this version of a British native plant. Its many slender stems carry small, dense spikes of pale pink flowers. *90 × 50*

—*vaccinifolium* is a hardy, prostrate, mat-forming perennial for the rock garden. It bears tiny oval leaves tinged with red above and miniature spikes of pink flowers appear from the leaf axils during the fall. *10 × 60*

Portulaca 133
P. grandiflora ('Sun plant') is a fleshy-leaved, short, bushy annual, the wild plants originally coming from Brazil. They bear large semi-double flowers in red, pink or yellow the whole summer long – but as their common name suggests only when the sun is shining! These plants are for hot dry positions as edging, on the rockery, dry bank or planter. Raise the seed under glass and plant them out during warm weather. *15 × 15*

Potentilla 141
Known as 'Cinquefoil', the herbaceous species of poten-tilla are easily grown border and rock plants. Any soil that does not dry out completely suits them and although they are generally planted in the sun some shade is tolerated. Their habit varies according to species but the taller growers can be rather sprawling with their strawberry-like flowers produced on stems that de-velop from silvery leaves.

Increase is by dividing the crowns during the fall.

—*alba* is a plant for the rock garden with neat growth bearing loose terminal clusters of white flowers. *10 × 15*

—*fragriformis* is one of the best known with low growth, grey woolly leaves and a few wide yellow flowers. *25 × 35*

— **'Gibson's Scarlet'** is a hybrid with single blood-red flowers in long succession. *30 × 35*

—*nepalensis* **'Miss Willmott'** has single bright rose-crimson flowers. *30 × 40*

—*recta* **'Warrenii'** has hairy leaves and stems on a bushy plant. The wide clear yellow flowers are carried in clusters. *45 × 45*

—*ternata* is a colourful rock plant arrayed with its deep yellow flowers through most of the summer. *10 × 20*

— × *tonguei* is a sprawling rock plant with upright stems bearing sparse clusters of yellow and orange flowers. *15 × 30*

—*verna* **'Nana'** forms a bright green tufted mat studded with tiny yellow blooms. This is small enough to be accommodated in a trough garden. *8 × 15*

Primula

Few gardeners are not familiar with at least some of this large genus. As well as the many species and their cultivars for woodland, streamside or rock gardens both 'Primrose' and 'Polyanthus' — so useful for bedding out, belong here too. To succeed, most primulas require a fertile, moist — yet free-draining-soil to which leaf-mould or peat has been added. Many are tolerant of some degree of shade particularly if the site is damp. All the species are raised from seed sown as soon after ripening as possible. These can be sprinkled on to pots of sandy compost and placed under a shaded garden light. Cultivars are increased by division of their crowns in late summer after flowering.

—*alpicola* bear dainty stems of scented flowers. They are normally seen as a mixture of colours: white, yellow, purple or violet. *30 × 30*

—**'Ashore Hybrids'** these are also in mixed colours with mauve-lilac predominating. This group was developed by crossing *P. beesiana* with *P. bulleyana*. *60 × 35*

—**'Aurantiaca Hybrids'** are mixed orange and yellow shades. *60 × 30*

—*auricula* is an old favourite which forms rosettes of often mealy leaves and has large flowers on short stems. In the wild plant these are yellow but, in the years since these plants have been cultivated, many choice kinds have been developed. The bulk of these are now, sadly, simply names in old books. Some named sorts are still available including 'Irish Blue' which has clear blue flowers. *15 × 15*

—*beesiana* is a bog primula with stout stems and whorls of rose-purple flowers. *50 × 35*

—*capitata mooreana* is an attractive kind which forms clumps of white-backed green leaves. The violet flowers appear rather later than most primula species. *20 × 25*

—'**Chungensis Hybrids**' have flowers in surprisingly rich orange shades. *40 × 30*

—*cockburniana* is a Chinese plant with stems of orange flowers. *10 × 15*

—*denticulata* is sometimes named the 'Drumstick primula' these bear ball-like heads of small flowers. Many colours are available including lilac, purple, red and 'Alba' pure white. *25 × 35*

—*florindae* ('Himalayan cowslip') is the giant of the group with thick stems each supporting a mop head of as many as 40 sweetly scented pale yellow flowers. The best plants will be seen near or actually in water. *75 × 40* **1**

—*frondosa* is an early flowering woodland or shade plant bearing pretty yellow-eyed rose-lilac flowers. *10 × 15*

—*helodoxa* is a most attractive species with whorls of yellow flowers. These are suited to planting in open woodland. *60 × 25* **145**

—*japonica* is another tall grower for planting near water. From the fresh green crowns appear stems of bright red flowers which are carried tier upon tier. *60 × 40* **149**

—×*juliana* This is the garden name (botanically *P. x pruhoniciana*) for a group of colourful low growing hybrids of *P. juliae*. The cultivar 'Betty Green' an early flowering crimson sort is an example. *10 × 20* **144**

—*marginata* forms clumps of mealy leaves from which spring stems of blue lilac flowers. *15 × 20*

—*polyneura* has soft downy leaves with stems of variable colour flowers, in the best form rich purple-red. *30 × 35* **146**

—*pulverulenta* are vigorous, easy plants for moist situations with tiered whorls of red flowers each with a deeper coloured eye. This is a parent of many fine hybrids. '**Bartley Strain**' is one of these with flowers in a mixture of white, pink and rose. *45 × 30*

—*rosea* 'Delight' bears clear rose flowers each with a distinct yellow eye. These appear with the new bronze-tinged leaves early in the spring. For a moist spot. *10 × 30*

—*secundiflora* bears clusters of drooping, purple flowers in early summer. *30 × 25*

—*sieboldii* These are very showy plants with creeping stems and tufts of downy leaves. Originally from Japan where several fine cultivars have been developed. They also make splendid pot plants for a cool greenhouse. *20 × 25*

—*sikkimensis* has strong stems bearing a mass of clustered yellow 'primroses' each held on a slender stalk. *30 × 25*

— × *variabilis* ('Polyanthus') are superb plants for winter and spring bedding displays. Treat the plants as biennials sowing the seed in early summer for planting out during the fall. 'Pacific Giants' are the favourite strain the world around with sturdy stems and large heads of clear colours. 'Pacific Dwarf Jewel' is a new development, almost intermediate between a polyanthus and a primrose when the first flowers appear.

Individually these are exceptionally large and include choice lavender and blue in the strain. *20 × 20* **147**

—*viali* is a distinct species which bears dense poker-like spikes of small bluish flowers. *45 × 30*

—*vulgaris* ('Primrose'). Very many different colours and forms of these familiar early spring flowering plants have been developed from the original wild sulphur-yellow colour. Use them for bedding, planters or rockery. 'Beidermeier' is a fine strain of selected colours produced on compact plants. *15 × 20*

Pulmonaria

The 'Lungwort' genus is comprised of low-growing herbaceous plants with broad, pointed, rather rough leaves varying in colour from green to grey and frequently spotted too. They are early spring flowering with small stems of clustered, tubular flowers. These are useful plants for ground cover in light shade, under shrubs, edgings or on the larger rock garden. Although reasonably tolerant of poor soil they respond to better conditions with more vigorous growth and consequently finer flowers the following season. Unless used as ground cover, for which incidentally they are invaluable, lungworts need dividing up after flowering every three to four years. After discarding the poor pieces the strong crowns can be replanted and kept watered until re-established.

— *angustifolia* ('Blue Cowslip') has clusters of intensely blue tubular flowers. *25 × 35*

— *officinalis* ('Lungwort') is one of the more frequently seen of the group. Its clusters of pink flowers have the intriguing habit of fading to lavender-blue. *30 × 40*

— *saccharata* **'Bowles Red'** has elliptical spotted leaves and fine sprays of light red flowers. *30 × 40*

Pulsatilla

The 'Pasque flower' a close relative of the anemone, produces stems of silky-haired buds. These open into cup-shaped flowers appearing with the emerging finely-cut leaves. The silken haired seed heads are also an attraction and they last on the plants for several weeks. The best soil for these choice plants is free-draining, firm, alkaline loam. A sunny position at the front of a border or on the rock garden suits them. New plants are easily raised if freshly ripe seed is sown as soon as possible, potting on the seedlings before they get too large. These are plants which resent disturbance, so site them well and leave undisturbed.

— *vulgaris* has flowers in delightful shades of mauve, white and red. *25 × 30*

Pyrethrum 143

P. roseum the garden 'Pyrethrum' is a clump-forming border plant with finely divided leaves and tall stems carrying solitary single or double daisy-like flowers. They are both fine border plants and good cut-flowers. A sunny position on light, fertile soil is best for these showy plants. Divison of the rather woody roots, each complete with a vigorous crown will provide new stock for planting. This is something which must be done after flowering every third season to prevent overcrowding of the centres.

—— **'Brenda'** is deep pink with

yellow centres. *75 × 45*

—— **'Bressingham Red'** is a good clear red. *75 × 45*

—— **'E. M. Robinson'** is light pink with a golden centre. *75 × 45*

—— **'Lord Roseberry'** has double red blooms. *60 × 54*

—— **'Vanessa'** also double, is rich pink. *60 × 45*

—— **'White Madelaine'** has large double white flowers. *60 × 45*

Rudbeckia 126, 151, 152

Colourful perennial and annual border plants originally from North America. They have large daisy-like blooms often yellow in colour each with a prominent central disc which suggested the common name, 'Coneflower'. All prefer a sunny position in well-drained, fertile soil which does not get too dry in hot weather as they are making their growth. An exception is the short-lived perennial species. *R. hirta* which we find is able to withstand drought conditions without flagging. Many kinds have long flower stems which makes them useful for cutting. Sow the seeds

of the annual kinds (and *R. hira* mentioned above) outside in late spring (or inside in cooler climates) and transplant the seedlings to their flowering positions when ready. The perennials can be increased by dividing their roots when dormant. Some light staking with twigs and garden twine may be advisable in order to keep their flowering stems up together.

The annuals have been developed from *R. bicolor* and *R. hirta*.

— **'Marmalade'** forms bushy plants for weeks smothered with stems of golden-orange flowers each with a black cone. *45 × 30*

— **'Tetraploid Giant Hybrids'** These bear extra large flowers in yellow, bronze and bicolours. *75 × 50*

— *hirta* ('Black-eyed Susan') is a favourite perennial with golden-yellow petals drooping from the central black cone. Hybrids come in single and double forms and as well as yellow there are bronze and mahogany shades. *60 × 40*

— *laciniata* is a tall back-of-the-border plant with smooth green leaves and tall stems of yellow flowers. *180 × 75*

——'**Goldquelle** has deep yellow double blooms. *90 × 60*

——'**Goldsturm**' is clear yellow but with dark centres. *75 × 50*

——'**Herbstsonne**' is another tall sort with yellow petals drooping from a central green cone. *150 × 75*

—*speciosa* is a much-branched border plant with black cones to its orange-yellow flowers. *90 × 60*

Salpiglossis

S. sinuata originally from Chile, are erect-growing annuals with an exotic appearance. Use these in pots or borders where their colourful trumpet-shaped flowers, often with throat and veining in a complementary shade, will surprise and entrance. From a single packet of seed you may expect to see deep blue with gold, lavender and black, red and gold or orange and so on. The seed should be sown under glass in early spring and pricked out into boxes or pots when large enough to handle. Pinching out the tips of young plants encourages bushiness. A sunny position in reasonably fertile soil will suit these. It is usual to give some support to the flowering stems. Two strains which we have grown are: 'Bolero' and 'Shalimar'. *60 × 30* **154**

Salvia

The 'Sages' are a very large and varied genus of plants containing annuals, perennials and shrubs. A fertile, well-prepared soil in full sun is required by all. The perennial species are good border plants. Many of them have blue flowers which contrast nicely with yellow flowered plants. Cuttings of soft new shoots can be rooted during the spring or summer. The tender perennials are normally treated as half-hardy annuals, discarding them at the end of the season.

—*farinacea* '**Blue Bedder**' is a compact, deep blue, flowered bedding plant. Although a perennial the plants are normally raised as half-hardy annuals. *75 × 60*

—*haematodes* is upright with showy spikes of violet-blue flowers. They are rather short-lived and normally increased by seed each year to flower the following season. *90 × 60*

—*horminum* is an annual originally from S. Europe long grown in gardens for the colourful topmost bracts which can be rose, purple, white or blue according to cultivar selected. *45 × 45*

—*patens* is an attractive half-hardy Mexican species once again frequently raised as an annual from an early sowing under glass. The flowers are either blue or white. *60 × 40*

—*sclarea* is a hardy biennial herb its dried leaves said to have a use in the flavouring of soups. We have not tried this but find the plant a useful addition to the mixed border or in isolation on the rock garden. The seeds may be sown outside during the spring preferably where they are to flower. Drastic thinning can take place as the youngsters develop. Pale rose-blue flowers follow in the plants' second season on stems up to 1m high. *90 × 30* **125**

—*splendens* is the brilliant-flowered 'Scarlet sage'. This is frequently planted in Britain in the patriotic colour scheme of red, white and blue (the other colours being provided by sweet alyssum and lobelia). There are several splendid strains available in varying heights to suit individual needs. They require a temperature of at least 18°C for regular germination. Once pricked out this can be lowered to 12°C for growing on. Do not plant these outside until the danger from late

frost is over. *25—40 × 30*

— × *superba* These hybrids form bushy clumps and bear upright stems of blue-purple flowers. Increase plants by division. *90 × 60*

Sanguisorba

These are also sometimes seen as *Poterium*. They are interesting if somewhat dull plants considering the range there are available. Although they can be used in the border their main value is in waterside planting where they can be grouped. Obviously moist soil is preferred so if planting in drier places ensure that plenty of humus is dug into the soil first. Division of the clumps during the dormant season is the way to increase your stock.

—*obtusa* is a Japanese species with pale green leaves and purple-pink, bottlebrush-like flowers. *90 × 45*

Saponaria

S. ocymoides ('Rock soapwort') is these days the most frequently seen of the genus. This has prostrate stems clad with grey-green leaves and loose sprays of light rose-pink flowers. As its common name suggests this is a plant for the rock garden and it is never better than when trailing down over rock face or filling a crevice. A sunny place in lime-free soil will grow the best plants. Propagation is from seed sown in pots and over wintered in a cold frame. *15 × 45*

———'**Bressingham**' is a very choice kind but rather slow to establish. Plant this in well-drained loam which has been top-dressed with fine gravel. The flowers are a clear bright pink. Raise new plants from cuttings. *5 × 25*

Saxifraga 3, 155

The 'Saxifrage' genus is a very large one in which the low growing mostly mountain plants fall naturally into different groups. In addition many of the species hybridise freely so that literally dozens of names are recorded for these crosses. Not all are freely available – the small selection listed below gives a cross section of those usually seen. Cultivation consists of providing a light gritty soil with the addition of peat or leafmould (few tolerate waterlogged conditions for

very long). The rock garden is the natural place for most in the list although some e.g. London pride, *Saxifraga umbrosa*, can also be used either as an edging or ground cover in light shade. We suggest that groups of not less than three clumps be placed together, spacing them according to vigour. Most non-flowering rosettes can be rooted easily if placed in pots of free-draining compost and these accommodated in a cold frame during the winter.

Encrusted section – these flower in summer and require a light (limy) soil in sun or light shade.

—*aizoon* '**Baldensis**' bears its dainty sprays of tiny white flowers which spring from dense hummocks of minute silvery foliage. *10 × 20*

———'**Lutea**' produces rosettes of light green leaves and stems of pale lemon flowers. *20 × 30*

———'**Rosea**' This version quickly forms clumps of silvery leaves and has pale rose flowers. *25 × 45*

—*cochlearis* '**Minor**' has white flowers springing from the hard mass of mounded silver rosettes. *12 × 20*

—**'Esther'** is a splendid quick growing hybrid with red speckled primrose colour flowers. *15 × 25*

—*lingulata* **'Albida'** has vigorous growing rosettes and long sprays of white flowers. *30 × 35*

—**'Whitehills'** is a neat grower with masses of white flowers on delicate stems. *15 × 25*

Cushion section – these flower in early spring and need a position where there is shelter from the mid-day sun. Well-drained moist soil.

—*apiculata* stems of pale primrose flowers develop from spiky green rosettes.

——**'Alba'** is an interesting white counterpart of the above. *10 × 20*

—**'Boston Spa'** This favourite has masses of clear yellow flowers. *8 × 15*

—**'Cranbourne'** bears relatively large blooms which spring from hard grey cushions. *3 × 15*

—**'Elizabethae'** has light yellow flowers and is one of the first to show colour early in the new year. *8 × 25*

— ×*irvingii* is very dense growing with pink/lilac almost stemless flowers. *10 × 20*

— ×*jenkinsae* with large pink blooms produced just above the foliage. *3 × 15*

S. Moschata or mossy section – these flower from early spring to early summer and prefer a moist spot in part shade. They will tolerate sun better if the soil remains moist.

—**'Cloth of Gold'** has clear gold rosettes – white flowers. An effective colour contrast when planted next to deeper tones. *10 × 20*

—**'Dubarry'** is a vigorous grower in which the light crimson flowers are well displayed against the rich green leaves. *15 × 30*

—**'Kingii'** Dense growing dwarf form with white flowers. *3 × 25*

—**'Pixie'** has tiny stems of clear pink blooms arranged on compact dome – like clumps. *3 × 30*

—**'Pipers Pink'** is of similar flower colour to the above but rather more vigorous in growth. *8 × 30*

—**'Triumph'** has rich red flowers produced with abandon. *15 × 30*

Miscellaneous section

—*fortunei* is a choice species from the Far East with glossy palmate leaves from amongst which arise thin stems of white flowers during the fall. They succeed best when planted in moist soil in a shady spot and for

215

winter protection need a light cover of bracken or leaves after their deciduous leaves die down. *30 × 25*

——**'Wada's variety'** This superb selection displays rich purple leaves which emphasise the pure whiteness of the blooms. *35 × 20*

—*oppositifolia* **'Latina'** is a refined version of the wild species which forms a mat of creeping stems and leaves. The large almost stemless flowers open wide early in the year. Rather moist but not stagnant gritty soil suits these best. *5 × 45*

— × *primulaize* A cool spot is needed for this plant of garden origin to display its short stems of salmon or orange flowers during the summer. *10 × 25*

—*umbrosa* ('London Pride') A familiar cottage garden plant with dark green rosettes which produce dainty sprays of pink flowers. *25 × 45*

——**'Primuloides, Elliots Variety'** We prefer this choice half size version of the above and love to see it taking over a shady nook in the rock garden. *8 × 30*

——**'Aurea Punctata'** has bold splashes of gold on the leaves which contrasts well with the normal dark green. Plant them in the sun for the best colour. *20 × 40*

Scabiosa

In Europe *S. caucasica* is both a familiar florist cut-flower and good border plant. They thrive in any well-drained soil (including lime) which should have some old manure or peat incorporated into it before the plants are first set out. Select a sunny place for the group where the long-stemmed, wide, single flowers will be produced over many weeks. Divide crowns in spring to obtain new plants.

——**'Bressingham White'** is a strong growing white. *60 × 45*

——**'Clive Greaves'** is the ever popular lavender-blue. *60 × 45*

Sidalcea

S. malvaeflora are neat growing plants with shiny green, rounded basal leaves and sturdy upright stems, topped with spikes of pretty mallow-like flowers. Whenever possible plant these in groups in fertile, well-drained loam either in the sun or part shade. New stock comes from dividing clumps in the spring.

——'**Croftway Red**' has clear rich red flowers. *90 × 45*

—— '**Loveliness** is a dense spiky grower with stems of shell-pink flowers. *75 × 45*

—— '**Rose Queen**' is a popular kind bearing pale pink blooms arranged in dainty spikes. *120 × 60*

——'**Wm. Smith**' is rich pink, similar type of growth although generally not as tall as the above. *90 × 45*

Silene
S. acaulis 'Moss campion, or Cushion pink', is a good garden representative of this large group of which few seem to be in cultivation. These are easily grown although in our experience not always too generous with their flowers unless ideally sited. Their native home is upon mountains of the N. Hemisphere where they naturally inhabit very gritty soil where some moisture is always available lower down. The plant is variable in the wild; one of the best sorts listed in nursery catalogues is *S. acaulis var excapa* which has clear pink stemless flowers. Increase these by dividing up the turf-like mat in spring. *8 × 25*

Soldanella
S. montana is a charming dwarf alpine plant. When grown in a cool spot in 'open' gritty soil forms spreading mats of glossy, rounded leaves. Fringed bell-shaped lavender flowers emerge during the spring from buds which were formed some time previously. A little protection in the form of a glass sheet may be required for these if the weather remains unduly wet for a length of time. To increase these choice plants the crowns may be very carefully divided after flowering. Seed can be sown in pans during the winter. *15 × 30*

Solidago
Many of the species of *Solidago* or 'Goldenrod' tend to be coarse growing and more suitable for the rough corners of the garden. The garden hybrids however come into a different category for these are much valued in the mixed border both for their late flowering and as a golden foil for the brighter colours. There

are both tall and compact growers all sharing the similar narrow green leaves and feathery plumes of tiny flowers. Goldenrod likes a slight well-drained soil either in the sun or tolerating part-shade. Manured ground, although not too important with these easy-to-grow plants, will ensure sturdy growth and good sprays of flowers. Watering during dry weather is also important and will ensure that the lower leaves remain fresh and green. Light staking of the taller kinds will keep the long stems headed in the right direction. Division must be done frequently say every 2 or 3 seasons. Strong crowns detached at that time provide new planting material.

— × *hybridus* is a group name normally used for all the garden hybrids. These are of differing heights, all have dense sprays of tiny yellow flowers.

——'**Cloth of Gold**' is dwarf growing with deep yellow flowers. *45 × 30*

——'**Crown of Rays**' has open, spreading flower clusters. *45 × 30*

——'**Goldenmosa**' is bushy with dense masses of flower. *75 × 45*

——'**Goldstrahl**' (Peter Pan) is an upright grower bearing light yellow blooms. *75 × 45*

——'**Golden Thumb**' produces its pale yellow sprays on small bushes. *30 × 25*

——'**Lemore**' is a mass of light yellow on spreading flower heads. *75 × 45*

——'**Mimosa**' is a mimosa-like golden yellow hybrid. *150 × 45*

Stachys

These are mat-forming perennials which are easily grown plants for ordinary soil in sun or part shade. Their flowers are carried in whorls on short, upright spikes. The two species below are increased by dividing the clumps during the spring and replanting the youngest portions.

—*lanata*. 'Lambs tongue' is the popular name for these low spreading plants with almost prostrate leaves which are thickly covered in soft silvery hairs. When used as summer bedding the woolly spikes of pale rose flowers are regarded as of secondary importance and, rather than allowing them to flower leaving bare patches, these are removed

218

as they appear. This is a good edging plant but not for cold wet soils, where they are short-lived. *30 × 45*

—*macrantha* is an upright grower with crinkly, rich green leaves. The clustered flowers are variable in colour, the cultivar 'Rosea' having good clear rose blooms. *45 × 40* **159**

Stokesia **157**

This genus comprises but one distinctive plant from N. America. *S. laevis*, or 'Stokes aster', is an erect growing border plant with cornflower-like blooms. If planted in a light well-drained soil in a sheltered position flowers may be expected from early summer through until the frosts. Water the clumps in dry weather and remove the dead heads to keep new blooms coming along. Seeds when sown under glass during early spring should ensure flowering plants for the following year. Alternatively, clumps may be divided in late spring. In cold areas a light covering of straw or dry litter over the partially evergreen leaves is suggested but this should only be required during severe con-

ditions. Various colour selections of the species are listed by nurserymen including:

——**'Blue Star'** which has wide lavender-blue flowers. *45 × 45*

——**'Wyoming'** rather deeper blue than the normal 'wild' colour. *45 × 45*

Tagetes **19, 161**

The African and French marigolds which have been derived from *T. erecta* and *T. patula* must be among the most widely grown of half-hardy annuals. When it comes to creating a quick, bright show of colour few plants are more reliable than the modern hybrids from these groups. Not everyone likes them of course and personally we do not care for the smell of the heavily scented foliage as it gets brushed against when weeding. The African marigold has large, dense almost ball-shaped flowers, in shades of yellow or orange, frequently on tall plants. French marigolds have more flowers which are smaller. These are sometimes striped or crested in darker colours, where the Africans are plain colours. As more hybrids are raised each year, the distinction between the groups tends to get less. A further plant of this genus grown in gardens is *T. tenuifolia* commonly referred to as tagetes. This has smaller flowers still and makes a neat edging plant. All of these may be raised from seed sown out-of-doors in a warm, well-drained soil. Most people, including the nurserymen, prefer to give them a good start in life by sowing them under glass and planting out when all frosts are over. Although a little tedious it is worth the effort to remove the faded flowers, particularly early in the season for an even brighter display later. Innumerable varieties are obtainable, for the names of which consult your seedsman's catalogue. The hybrids now being offered are superior in vigour, uniformity and ability to flower sooner and longer than earlier strains.

— 'Climax Mixed' are tall African marigolds with massive flowers in favourite colours. *90 × 45*

— 'Gay Ladies' are also Africans with large blooms in shades of lemon, orange yellow and gold on compact plants. *35 × 45*

— 'Golden Jubilee' holds its large golden blooms well clear of the foliage. *70 × 45* **162**

— 'Moonshot' is an early flowering African which produces clear, light yellow blooms on compact bushes. *30 × 40*

— 'Paprika' (*T. tenuifolia* hybrid) is usually listed in seed catalogues as *Tagetes signata pumila* which, in spite of its big name, is a tiny plant with bushy growth, bearing masses of dark brown-red single blooms. A fine edging plant for poor soil. *15 × 20*

— 'Petite' strain are mini-size French marigolds which are available in separate colours. The plants are neat and compact – very free-flowering. *15 × 20*

— 'Susanna' 'Red Brocade' is a French type with striking gold-edged mahogany-red single flowers. *35 × 40* **130**

Thalictrum 78

Known as 'Meadow rue' the plants of this genus number over one hundred species but few of these are worthwhile to be in general cultivation. Those that are grown vary considerably in height ranging from a few cms up to nearly

2m. All share the attractive delicate leaves composed of several leaflets – reminiscent of Maidenhair fern – and the tiny flowers are usually arranged on loose heads. Both leaves and flowers find favour for floral work. They are hardy plants succeeding in normal garden soil. Tall sorts can go in at the rear of the mixed border, either in the sun or light shade. They require watering during a dry spell. Cut the old flowering stems right down after the stamens fall. The dwarf kinds are best on a sunny rockery where they can be allowed to spread and form a good clump. All will benefit from a top-dressing of compost now and then. Normally the plants should only be lifted when stock, endeavour to obtain pot-quired as older clumps may be difficult to re-establish once again. New plants are obtained by division of the fibrous roots before or after flowering. When purchasing your initial stock, endeavour to obtain pot-grown specimens.

— *aquilegiifolium* is an ornamental species for the border with large greyish leaves and loose panicles of purplish anthers. *120 × 60*

— *dipterocarpum* grows best where the soil never dries out completely. Its tall stems of yellow centred mauve flowers need staking to stop them toppling over. *150 × 60*

— — **'Hewitts Double'** although not as tall as the species, still requires support for its small rootstock and can be damaged if the plant gets wind rocked. This is a choice sort which should be in everyone's border. It bears masses of double mauve flowers. *90 × 60*

— *kiusianum*. Originally from S. Japan this species is one of the smallest in its genus. Plant a group of these on the rock garden and they will spread a little by means of underground runners if the position is to their liking. *10 × 25*

— *minus* is the name given to an extremely variable group. Many of those normally seen are dwarf with very divided leaves – flowers are of little merit. The foliage when cut is most useful for placing with other flowers. Hence its inclusion here! *25 × 35*

Thymus 160

'Thyme' is the name for a group of numerous small shrublets including the culinary herb with aromatic leaves. They are of compact upright growth and also include some prostrate spreading species described briefly below. We have added these as they are invaluable on the rock garden or for filling pockets in crazy paving. Acid or alkaline soil appears to be immaterial to the successful cultivation of the carpenters, although it should be well-drained and in a sunny place. Division of the plants is easy as the stems self-root as they touch the soil. Spring made cuttings also root readily in sandy compost.

—*serpyllum* is the name given for the variable, free-flowering prostrate garden forms.

——**'Albus'** has white flowers in a carpet of light green leaves. *3 × 40*

——**'Annie Hall'** bears masses of shell-pink flowers. *3 × 40*

——**'Coccineus'** is red-pink, the most intense colour. *5 × 45*

——**'Major'** is larger growing but otherwise similar to 'Coccineus'. *8 × 60*

——**'Minor'** has pale pink flowers and is the mini of the group. *2 × 30*

——**'Pink Chintz'** is a mat of grey leaves studded with pink flower clusters. *5 × 45*

Tierella 158

The two species of 'Foam flower' below are low growing North American plants with soft green leaves and foam-like sprays of tiny flowers. Blooming for several weeks from late spring on, they are much valued for massing in part shade at the edge of a shrub border or on the shady rock garden. They are easy to grow in most soils but add humus if the ground is stony. Division of the plants in spring or fall is the way to increase your stock.

—*cordifolia* is a rampant weed-smotherer when well nourished spreading its stolons in all directions. The plumes of tiny cream flowers are carried well above the dense foliage. *15 × 60*

—*wherryi* is clump forming with slightly pink-tinged white flowers over golden green leaves. This is a first choice for a partly shaded peat bed. *15 × 45*

Tradescantia 163

T. virginiana ('Spider-wort') is a hardy perennial for the border with soft, rush-like leaves and 3-petalled flowers which open in succession from the mass of buds present. There are several colours available in these plants which are related to the tender indoor tradescantias including: purple, red, mauve, blue and white. They are herbaceous and may be propagated by division after their dead growth has been cut down in their dormant months. Slugs devour or damage their tender emerging shoots and must be dealt with by putting down slug pellets. *45 × 45*

Trollius

With its globular yellow or orange flowers and deeply cut palmate leaves the 'Globe flower' could be mistaken for a giant buttercup of which they are close relatives. These are sturdy, erect plants flourishing in damp ground including heavy clay if it is well provided with humus. Sun or part shade suits equally well. Removing the flowers as they fade often results in a second blooming. The clumps should be lifted and divided every third year and the propagated pieces replanted in manured ground.

We find that spring, just as the first pieces of green appears on the clump is a good time to carefully divide the wiry roots.

—**europaeus 'Superbus'** is a neat grower with pale yellow cup-like flowers and is a fine form of the Globe flower which occurs in upland meadows over much of Europe. *75 × 30*

— × *hybridus* The showy flowers of the garden forms appear in late spring to early summer on plants that are hybrids between two or more species from Europe and Asia.

——**'Alabaster'** has pale ivory-yellow flowers. *45 × 35*

——**'Bees Orange'** has large orange blooms in early summer. *40 × 45*

——**'Earliest of All'** bears large clear yellow orbs in early spring. *75 × 45*

——**'Goldquelle'** is a sturdy grower with pure yellow blooms. *75 × 45*

——**'Orange Princess'** produces tall stems of orange-yellow blooms. *90 × 45*

——**'Prichards Giant'** has vigorous growths topped with flowers of rich yellow. *90 × 45*

—*pumilus* **'Wargrave'** is a compact grower for the rock

223

garden or front of the border with many small yellow flowers. *30 × 40*

Ursinia 167

These garden hybrids with single, bright, calendula-like flowers are suitable for sunny beds or borders. They are half-hardy annuals originally derived from *U. Anethoides* a South African species. If a well-drained soil is chosen which is to the plants liking they will furnish a display which will last for weeks. Seeds should be sown where the plants are to flower, thinning them as required. An alternative method is to raise the young plants initially under glass, planting them outside when frosts are over. *30 × 35*

Verbascum

From a rosette of often densely hairy leaves will develop the upright spike of single flowers which are characteristic of the 'Mullein' clan. Some are very tall with imposing spires – others smaller, but all are most attractive border plants associating well with delphiniums and lupins. Several species have apparently contributed to the attractive garden hybrids. Sunny, rather dry borders in soil enriched with well decayed manure or compost suits them best. Few can tolerate wet conditions although if your soil is chalky they will have no objection. The named hybrids require to be perpetuated by cuttings – in this case root-cuttings. These are started in a cold frame and once they have formed a suitable rosette of leaves can be planted out. Seed germinates readily but does not come 'true' to name.

— 'Cotswold Beauty' has biscuit-colour flowers with pink anthers. *90 × 30*

— 'Cotswold Gem' is buff with rose shading and purple spots. *90 × 30*

— 'Gainsborough' produces a rosette of grey foliage and spikes of sulphur-yellow flowers. *120 × 35*

— 'Golden Bush' has bright yellow flowers in succession. *60 × 45*

— 'Mont Blanc' has dull green rather hairy leaves and stems of pure white blooms. *120 × 45*

— 'Pink Domino' has tapering spires of deep rose-pink flowers.

Verbena

These are a group of colourful, low-growing mostly half hardy bedding and rock plants. In the warmer temperate countries where only slight frosts occur the verbenas are put to good use as ground cover. These plants were formerly regarded as tender perennials in places where winter temperatures drop too low for the plants to remain outside. They were propagated by taking cuttings and keeping these in a heated glasshouse over the winter period. These days most of the plants of *V.* × *hybrida*, (Garden verbena) are raised anew each year by sowing seeds under glass during the early spring, boxing them up and later planting them out. The old plants are subsequently discarded at the end of the season. Although seed germination can be rather erratic, the colours obtained by this method are in a wide variety and of a quality similar to that of the named sorts. The plants are spreading, often rooting at the nodes as their stems touch the soil. For close carpet ground cover this trait can be encouraged if the stems are pegged down. The flowers, some of which are delicately scented, are individually like tiny primroses. They are produced in small heads and are in many shades of red, violet, pink, striped and white. An open, sunny position with the free-draining soil slightly enriched with rotted vegetable material will provide the best conditions for these colourful bedding plants which deserve more widespread planting.

— —'Blaze' is a seed-raised sort with bright scarlet flowers. *18 × 35*

— — 'Lawrence Johnson' is a superior cv with extra large trusses of vivid scarlet flowers. This is one of the kinds which has to be perpetuated by taking cuttings each year. *18 × 35*

— *chamaedrifolia* (*V. peruviana*) are low growing with many trusses of showy bright scarlet flowers which open in succession from late spring until fall. Frequently sold as rock plants they are by no means hardy and the long rooting stems should have some kind of protection during severe weather. *10 × 60*

— *venosa* (correctly, *V. rigida*) is

225

a popular, rather tender bedding plant with upright spikes bearing clusters of magenta flowers. Although perennial these can be raised from seed each year. 25 × 35

Veronica

The 'Speedwells' are a large group of generally easy-to-please plants. Some of the dwarf species are suited for planting on rock gardens or edging beds, the taller sorts are at home in the herbaceous or mixed border. Most grow well in normal garden soil although excessively dry places must be avoided. Propagation consists of dividing the clumps when they are dormant; small growers root from cuttings taken during the summer.

— *cinerea* is a grey-leaved carpet plant for the rock garden. It bears erect spikes of rose flowers. 10 × 30

— *gentianoides* is a pretty plant originally from the Caucasus which develops into a glossy-leaved mat sending up dainty spikes of light blue flowers during the early part of the summer. 30 × 45

— *incana* has long silver-grey leaves and dense, upright racemes of deep blue florets. 30 × 40

—— 'Wendy' has the same grey foliage but with deep lavender flowers. 50 × 30

— *longifolia* is a tall grower with toothed green leaves and long racemes of bluish flowers. 60 × 35

— *prostrata* is a free-flowering rock plant which forms a mat of stems with ascending flower spikes. Kinds available include:

—— 'Blue Sheen' which is a bright blue trailer. 10 × 35

—— 'Loddon Blue' with deep blue flowers. 10 × 35

—— 'Mrs. Holt' has flesh-pink flowers. 15 × 30

— *spicata* cultivars of this upright growing border species are available in shades of blue or pink and white. 45 × 30

— *teucrium* 'Crater Lake Blue' is a plant for grouping near the front of a border. We find that the rich blue flowers are particularly effective when contrasted with adjacent plants with yellow foliage. 30 × 30

— *virginiana* 'Alba' has tall, slender, unbranched stems bearing whorled leaves and spikes of white flowers. 150 × 35

Viola 156, 165

This genus of garden flowers which although botanically

226

known as *Viola* are more familiar as 'Violet', 'Viola' and 'Pansy'. Except for the few rock garden species grown, today's plants are the result of much hybridising. This group are short-lived perennials. The pansies in particular are often treated as annuals, raised from seed each year and then discarded. These must be everyone's favourites the world over with their masses of blooms in single and mixed colours, and frequently scented too. Seed may be sown either in the open ground during the spring or if early plants are wanted – under glass. Sun or part shade suits them if they are planted in moist, fertile, well-drained loam. Remember to remove the faded blooms to prolong their flowering. Another group of pansies, sometimes called 'Tufted pansies', are the violas (*V. williamsii*). These are scarcely different in general appearance and were originally raised about the middle of the last century by crossing the Garden pansies (*V. × wittrockiana*) with *Viola cornuta*. The plants tend to be longer lasting and are most effective when massed in beds, making good ground cover beneath roses for example. New stock of named kind are, unlike pansies, grown from cuttings – preferably from their basal shoots. Take these in early summer or fall, remove the lower leaves and place the prepared cuttings in a lightly shaded frame for rooting to take place. *Viola cornuta* together with its hybrid offspring bear masses of very dainty flowers. They are valued for edging beds or rock garden plantings. Propagation of these is either by dividing the partly rooted shoots from the clumps or sowing seed. The species has deep lavender flowers and there is an attractive white counterpart to the 'Alba'. 'Jersey Gem' with rich violet-blue flowers is an example of one of the hybrids of this section. 'Sweet violet', (*Viola odorata*): commercially grown bunches of sweet smelling violets are more frequently seen than the growing plants. These will grow into leafy patches in part shade. Their flowers which appear from late winter on have been evolved into many different colours from the original violet. They can now be had in pink, pale yellow, blue and white. Sometimes they are in single and double forms.

—*hederacea* is an example of the choice rock plants contained in the genus. A native of Australia it bears dainty flowers of violet with an edging of white for many weeks during the summer. A cool moist spot for this one. *10 × 30*

—*labradorica* is another choice rock species. This has heart-shaped leaves and tiny, white-throated violets when planted in the shade. *10 × 25*

Zinnia 164, 166

Few flowers have in recent years received quite the attention from hybridisers in selection and breeding of new plants as that of *Z. elegans*, a naturally variable Mexican species. The result being that there are now available to the home gardener a unique range of colours, heights and forms never before seen. There are Cactus-, Dahlia-, Scabious-, and Chrysanthemum-flowered – even one with green flowers (aptly named 'Envy'!). These colourful plants are annuals requiring a rich, light soil, well-drained – yet not drying out. In cool climates seed should be sown under glass. Do not sow these too early for seedlings are prone to a number of diseases if not growing strongly and once stunted with cold or damp seldom recover and make up into good plants. The alternative method is to sow the seed outside when night temperatures are in the $16°C – 18°C$ range. We always try to vary the planting site of this group from year to year in order to lessen the risk of disease transmission to the young plants. Hot, dry summers always suit the zinnias well. Our photograph taken in the Auckland City Council's Albert Park was the scene halfway through one of the hottest, driest seasons on record. Water restrictions meant that they could only receive a small amount of water through a hand-held hose. For a complete range of types and colours consult your seedsman's catalogue.

——'**Fruit Bowl**' has huge flowers with curled petals. *85 × 30*

——'**Peter Pan**' is a strain in an outstanding colour range with the large blooms produced on young plants. 25 × 20

—— **'Sombrero'** has flowers composed of red petals with gold tips – in appearance they are just like miniature Mexican hats! 60 × 45

—— **'State Fair Mixed'** have extra large dahlia-type blooms in a good range of colours. 75 × 45

—— **'Thumbelina'** is a mixed strain in which the compact plants bear tiny double and semi-double blooms. 20 × 20

GLOSSARY

Acid (soil)   Lime-free

Alkaline (soil)   Containing lime or chalk

Ascending   Curving upwards

Axil   The angle between stems and branchlet or branchlet and leaf

Break   To branch; send out new growth from dormant rootsock; mutate

Clone   Line of identical plants derived from a single original by vegetative means

Compost   Formulated mixture of soils used for potting or seed raising, *see also Garden compost*

Corolla   Collective term for the petals

Cultivar   From *culti*vated *var*iety, an internationally accepted term used for 'man-maintained variants'

Cultivar name   The name given to garden plants in the above category, recognised by its inclusion in single quotes

Evergreen   Leaves retained the year-round

Garden compost   Correctly rotted down garden refuse

Genus   A group (of plants in this case) which share close botanical similarities

Generic name   The first part of a plant's botanical Latin name

Glaucous   Foliage or stems having a covering of 'bloom', usually grey or bluish

Herbaceous   Dying to the ground annually

Hybrid   In the botanical sense a cross between two species (or genera), which is in the text printed as an × between (or before) the generic and specific names. Additionally the word hybrid is used for crosses

between cultivars of the same species. In the
descriptions those cvs with a single dash preceding
their name may be regarded as being of hybrid
origin.

Humus   Powder-like particles in the soil derived from
decayed vegetable matter

Inflorescence   The complete flower

Lateral   Emerging from the side

Light or Cold light   Glazed garden frame

Nodding   Hanging

Node   Leaf joint

Pendulous   Drooping downwards

Prostrate   Lying flat on the ground

Pyramidal   Broad-based tapering evenly toward the tip

Sepal(s)   Outer part of the flower

Species   Group of plants all with identical characteristics
which are maintained from generation to
generation; wild plants

Specific name   Second part of a plant's botanical Latin
name

Sport   Bud or seedling mutation which differs from its
parent as a result of genetic change, frequently the
source of a new cultivar

Stolons   Underground creeping shoots

Strike   To root

Stool   The special name for a rootstock of the chrysanthemum

Note on Descriptions pages 121–229

The genera (large bold headings) are listed in alphabetical
order. The descriptions of the genera are followed by brief
details of the species, hybrids and cultivars in smaller type. See
glossary notes.

Use of Dashes   One dash stands for the generic name in the
heading immediately above, the second dash for the species
name above-mentioned.

INDEX OF LATIN NAMES

Index of generic names of plants described. Numbers in **bold** type refer to the colour illustrations.

INDEX OF ENGLISH COMMON NAMES

Numbers in **bold** type refer to the colour illustrations.